Becky Fautz

Donna deVarona

GOLD MEDAL SWIMMER

Doubleday Signal Books

BONNIE

PONY OF THE SIOUX

THE JUNGLE SECRET

NORTH POLE: The Story of Robert E. Peary

BASEBALL BONUS KID

CAROL HEISS: Olympic Queen

GREEN LIGHT FOR SANDY

SEA TREASURE

THE BLOOD RED BELT

KENDALL OF THE COAST GUARD

RODEO ROUNDUP

NANCY KIMBALL, NURSE'S AIDE

FOOTBALL FURY

CIVIL WAR SAILOR

DINNY AND DREAMDUST

AUSTIN OF THE AIR FORCE

THE LONG REACH

FOOTLIGHTS FOR JEAN

BASEBALL SPARK PLUG

RUNAWAY TEEN

LIGHTNING ON ICE

HOT ROD THUNDER

JUDY NORTH, DRUM MAJORETTE

DIRT TRACK DANGER

ADVENTURE IN ALASKA

CLIMB TO THE TOP

FISHING FLEET BOY

JACK WADE, FIGHTER FOR LIBERTY

THE MYSTERY OF HIDDEN HARBOR

SCANLON OF THE SUB SERVICE

A SUMMER TO REMEMBER

NAT DUNLAP, JUNIOR "MEDIC"

BLAST-OFF! A Teen Rocket Adventure

TWO GIRLS IN NEW YORK

THE MYSTERY OF THE FLOODED MINE

CATHY AND LISETTE

EVANS OF THE ARMY

HIGH SCHOOL DROP OUT

DOUBLE TROUBLE

PRO FOOTBALL ROOKIE

THE MYSTERY OF BLUE STAR LODGE

ADVENTURE IN DEEPMORE CAVE

FAST BALL PITCHER

HI PACKETT, JUMPING CENTER

NURSE IN TRAINING

SHY GIRL: The Story of Eleanor Roosevelt

SKI PATROL

BIG BAND

GINNY HARRIS ON STAGE

GRACIE

THREE CHEERS FOR POLLY

TV DANCER

FEAR RIDES HIGH

THE MYSTERY OF THE INSIDE ROOM

ARTHUR ASHE: Tennis Champion

THE MYSTERY OF THE THIRD HAND SHOP

ROAR OF ENGINES

GOING, GOING, GONE

SECOND YEAR NURSE

GANG GIRL

THE KID FROM CUBA: Zoilo Versalles

DONNA DEVARONA

Donna deVarona

GOLD MEDAL SWIMMER

By Bob Thomas

DOUBLEDAY & COMPANY, INC.
GARDEN CITY, NEW YORK

FOREWORD

There are many times when a champion must be alone, for there is room at the top for only one. Sometimes being judged "the best" can be the loneliest thing in the world, but if someone is as fortunate as I have been, then these minutes of being set apart, completely on one's own, have been a small price to pay.

I would like to speak of—and to—my family, my coaches, and all of those people who, throughout my career, have taken time to write me a note or give me much-needed advice. Whenever the going got tough and I would begin to lose confidence in myself and in people, I would remind myself of all the wonderful people who had faith in me. I wished then that I could have answered these people. I hope that my gratitude can, in some measure, be expressed through this book. It is dedicated to you.

I cannot help but once again mention my coaches, who have in both negative and positive ways made me realize what the game is. Nor can I forget my

Mom, who never failed to get up at any odd hour to feed me before a 6 A.M. work-out. Or my Dad, who gave me so much confidence in myself that half the time I found myself in a race I had no right to be swimming. And my brother, Dave, and my sister, Jeanne, and, of course, little Kurt, who have all had to sacrifice for me and my career—and have done so willingly. Without these loving people I could never have achieved the things I did. I would never have had the strength or confidence to learn what it means to cope with victory and defeat, to realize that anything in life takes work. Life is a series of struggles; once one struggle is over, you prepare for the next one. To try to avoid struggle is trying to avoid life itself. Therefore, it is better to be defeated than not to know defeat—one must taste this before one can appreciate victory. Even victory is a relative term, for it can also become one's defeat. Thank you for reading my story.

Donna E. deVarona

CONTENTS

CONTENTS

GLOSSARY OF SWIMMING TERMS
USED IN THIS BOOK

back stroke—free style (see below) except for body position in water: this stroke is done while the swimmer is on his back.

breast stroke—body face down in water, legs straight and together, arms forward, palms of hands down; arms are pulled down and backward until elbows are at right angles to body, then elbows move down as if trying to squeeze the water from between arms and body; legs are drawn up, then pushed out powerfully with feet apart, soles flat against the water.

butterfly—body face down in water; arm stroke is like that of free style (see below) but done with both arms at the same time; kick is like free-style kick, but with both legs working together; arms and legs must both work at the same time.

flat-handed turn—swimmer helps himself to turn around in water by pressing the palm of his hand against the edge of the pool and pushing.

flip turn—a somersault in the water.

free style (also called the crawl)—body face down in water; arms work alternately, rising out of the water from the shoulder and reaching forward, then pulling down through the water and returning to first position; kick is an up-and-down motion with legs close together but not touching; there are six up-and-down beats of the legs to each complete arm stroke.

individual—race in which the swimmer may use any stroke he chooses.

lap—one length of the pool; if the race is 400 yards and the pool 50 yards long, each swimmer will swim 8 laps.

meter—a measurement; a meter is 39.37 inches long.

nationals—meets in which swimmers from all parts of the country compete.

relay race—a race in which several swimmers take part; each swims one lap.

CHAPTER 1

"AS WELL AS ANY BOY"

"Play ball!"

It was the beginning of a Little League game. The players in their slightly too-big uniforms trotted onto the dusty field and took their positions, as serious as the New York Yankees in a World Series.

"All right! Easy outs coming up!" shouted the boy on first, who seemed to feel responsible for providing the enthusiasm for the Lafayette Tigers.

"Give it to them, babe," he called to the pitcher, who was thumping the baseball into a glove that was nearly falling off his hand.

The Lafayette Giants were first at bat, and the short stop approached home plate with no signs of fear. The pitcher wound up and threw the ball. It never reached the catcher. The short stop swung hard, and the ball floated over the fence and into a pasture where cows were calmly chewing on clover. That was only the beginning. Before their half of the inning was over, the Giants were ahead 13 to 0.

At bat, the Tigers proved even more fumbling than they had been in the field and came up with three straight strike-outs. Then the Giants quickly raised the score to 27 to 0.

That was as much as Donna deVarona could stand.

For weeks she had been willing, if not content, to sit on the bench with her brother Deet and his dozen team mates. (Deet's real name was David T. deVarona, Jr. But it was too confusing to call him by his father's name, and he didn't like being called Junior, so he had settled for the first letters of his first and middle names.)

Deet was twelve and Donna was only nine, and he didn't particularly like a kid sister trailing after him. He had been especially upset when Donna announced that she was going to try out for the Little League team on which he played.

It wasn't that she didn't play well enough—she could hit a ball as far as many of Deet's pals. But a girl on a Little League team! That would have been more than Deet and his fellow players could bear, and they were happy when her application was denied.

They were not entirely pleased when Donna was allowed to become the bat boy—or bat girl—for the Lafayette Giants. But Donna was delighted. If she couldn't play for the team—a silly rule, she thought—she could at least be close to the action. She took her job seriously, lining the bats up in a neat row and picking up those that were dropped by batters after their turn at the plate.

But now when the Giants had reached such a huge lead over the Tigers, she could stand it no longer. "Let me bat," she whispered to her brother.

"What?" he said.

"Let me take a turn at bat," she urged. "I can get a hit—you know I can. I can hit almost as well as any boy on the team. Ask the manager to let me bat."

"Girls don't play in Little League," Deet reminded her with scorn.

"But they don't have to know I'm a girl," said Donna. "Look!" She tucked her blond curls under her baseball cap. "See—nobody will know the difference."

"You are a girl and everybody knows it," Deet insisted. "Now stop being silly and go pick up that bat."

Donna walked slowly to the plate and lifted the bat that had been dropped by a player who had just knocked out a three-base hit. She had been defeated in her plan to be "one of the boys." She sat sadly through the following innings, watching as the score advanced to Giants 38, Tigers 4. She couldn't understand why the boys would pass up an expert hitter just because she happened to be a girl.

But her unhappiness was only temporary. She loved Lafayette, a sunny little town in the hills east of San

Francisco Bay. She enjoyed it much more than San Francisco, where she had lived from the time she was three until she was six.

Donna had not been healthy in those San Francisco days. She was always suffering from sore throats in the fog and chill of San Francisco. That was one of the reasons why her father, an insurance man, had moved his wife and two children east to Lafayette, before the baby, Joanne, was born. Another reason for the move was to give Donna and Deet more room to move about outdoors. A big city is no fun for children, Mr. deVarona reasoned.

He was right. The move to Lafayette opened a whole new world for the young deVaronas. Now Donna had hills to climb and valleys to explore, and she spent long sunny summer days outdoors. Her health became better, and her small frame began to fill out. Indeed, thought her father, who was expert in such matters, she might even be made into an athlete.

"Donna!"

As she watched her brother cross home plate for the fifth time, she heard her father calling her. The sound brought mixed feelings. She adored her father, and yet she dreaded his reason for calling her.

"Donna! Time for your diving lesson!"

"Yes, Dad," she answered. "I'm coming."

She said good-by to the Little League players, extending the farewells as long as possible. Then she joined her father, who was waiting on the side lines. On the way to the car, she took off the baseball uniform, which she wore proudly in spite of the zero on the back that showed her position as bat girl. Underneath the uniform she was wearing the swim suit she used for diving practice.

Climbing into the front seat of the car, Donna sighed as her father drove off. "I wish," she thought, "that something would happen so I wouldn't have to go to diving practice. Oh, nothing bad! But couldn't the radiator boil over? Or couldn't we have a flat tire?"

Anything would do—as long as she didn't have to climb up on that high diving board. She was afraid. But it was a secret fear, one she couldn't bear to share with her father or the diving coach. They were so proud of her, she simply couldn't spoil everything by saying, "I'm afraid!" out loud. Besides, she was ashamed of her fear. She hated to admit that she was afraid of anything. But . . . that diving board was so high, and the water was so far, far down below!

The deVarona car pulled up in front of the swimming pool. Nothing had happened. She would have to take her diving lesson.

Her coach, Frank McGuigan, was waiting. "Hi, Donna," he said. "How's my prize pupil today?"

"Fine, thanks." But Donna realized as soon as she had spoken that she didn't sound fine. She hoped her father and the coach hadn't caught the downbeat tone of her voice.

The coach gave her a sharp look, but all he said was, "Take a few dives off the low board to warm up, Donna."

She walked to the deep end of the pool and began diving off the low board. She didn't mind that. It was the high board that made her breath hard to catch and her knees feel as if they had no bones in them.

Coach McGuigan turned to Mr. deVarona. "What's the matter with Donna?"

"What do you mean?" Mr. deVarona asked.

"She doesn't seem to be as interested in diving as she was at first. She was willing and eager when she started taking lessons. But lately I get the feeling that something is bothering her."

Mr. deVarona nodded. "You may be right. Usually she talks my ear off on the way here, but the past few times she's hardly said a word."

"I wonder if we are pushing her too hard."

"But didn't you say that's what we have to do, if she's going to be a champion?"

"Yes."

Mr. deVarona's eyes turned to his daughter, then back to the coach.

"Do you think she's got what it takes, Frank?"

"Yes, I think she has. She has 'good toes,' and

that's what we look for in top divers. It means her legs follow a good line, right to the point. Donna is as natural a diver as I have ever had for a student."

"But you yourself have told me that it takes more than being a natural to become a champion."

"It takes a lot of hard work," the coach agreed. "Plus one other thing, Dave."

"What's that?"

"She has to *want* it."

Donna was climbing out of the pool after her third practice dive. Coach McGuigan walked toward her to begin the lesson, and Mr. deVarona took a seat in the stands.

Donna went to work, performing a jack knife dive over and over again off the low board, perfecting each movement under the coach's instructions. She enjoyed this part of the lessons. She liked the all-in-one-piece feeling her body had when her dive was just right. And she enjoyed the look of approval in the coach's eyes, the smile on her father's face.

The hot August sun was beginning to drop toward the West as the coach said, "All right, Donna, let's have a few dives off the high board, then we will call it quits for today."

Donna stood still. This was the bad moment in every diving practice. And this time, she didn't think she could face it. She wasn't at all sure she could make herself walk to the high board, climb the ladder.

And that was the easy part. After that came the long dive! "I've got to," her stubbornness argued inside her, but her fear answered, "I can't!"

"I—I don't want to," she heard herself say out loud.

Surprise showed in the coach's eyes. "Oh, come on, Donna. It's nothing to worry about. You've done it before. The water's awfully soft to land on."

Donna couldn't make herself move. "I don't want to," she repeated.

The coach looked toward Mr. deVarona, who got up and came over. "Now, honey, you have to do what the coach tells you," he said to Donna. "That's the only way you are going to be a good diver."

Donna looked toward the high board, which seemed to tower above her. She walked slowly toward it and began climbing the ladder. With each step she felt sicker in her stomach. She reached the top and looked down, and her head whirled. She was on the ten-foot board—twelve and a half feet above the water—but it seemed three or four times higher. She tried not to look down.

"All right, Donna," called the coach. "Let's see you do the one-and-a-half flip."

She hesitated, and he called out: "You can do it. You've done it before. Get a good bounce on the board and don't forget to point those toes."

There was no turning back, not with her father watching her, his face anxious. To climb back down the ladder would have been a defeat for her and a disappointment for him. There was nothing to do but dive. *Don't think about how you feel—just dive.*

Donna measured off the steps to the end of the board, then stood at perfect attention, arms stiff by her sides. She took the few steps, lifted one leg and rose into the air. Down she came and the board dipped beneath her, then rose again. Now she was in the air and ready to do the flip.

At first her form was perfect. Then in a split second something went wrong. Just the slightest arm movement disturbed her balance and she lost her control. She could not complete the flip, and she landed on her back with a great splash.

Donna's father rushed to the edge of the pool. Donna rose to the surface and tried to smile to show that she was all right.

"I think we had better quit for today, Frank," Mr. deVarona said.

"Yes, she's had enough," the coach agreed.

Donna was silent on the drive home. The stinging of her skin had stopped, but her back felt bruised. Worse than that, she felt she had failed her father, and that hurt more.

Deet was full of talk about the Little League game at dinner, but Donna scarcely said a word. Her stomach still felt jumpy, and she picked at her food.

Finally her mother said, "Donna, you are not eating. Aren't you feeling well?"

"I'm tired and I don't feel hungry," Donna replied. "May I be excused, please?"

"Of course, dear," said her mother. "Why don't you go to your room and get into bed? You'll feel better with some rest."

After Donna had left the room, Mrs. deVarona asked her husband, "What's the matter with her? She's usually so gay at the dinner table. It isn't like her to be tired."

"Oh, she had a bad work-out at diving this afternoon," said Mr. deVarona. "It's nothing. She's bound to have an off day now and then."

But when he passed the door of Donna's bedroom later that evening, he could hear her crying softly. He opened the door and saw her stretched out on the bed with her head in the pillow. Her body shook with sobs.

Mr. deVarona hurried to her and wrapped his arms around her. "What's the matter, honey?" he asked.

The answer burst out. "I don't want to dive, Daddy. It scares me."

Her father rocked her back and forth to stop her crying, just as he had done when she was a baby. "There, there," he said. "You don't have to dive if you don't want to. You don't have to do anything you are afraid of."

Gradually her sobbing stopped. He dried her face and sat beside her on the bed.

"I didn't know you felt that way about diving," he told her. "I certainly wouldn't have had you do it if I had known. But you see, Donna, you have a certain gift. I recognized it, and so did Coach McGuigan. It's something that very few girls have. Do you understand what I'm talking about?"

"No," Donna admitted.

"I'm talking about the gift that God has given you of a fine body and the ability to make it move easily and gracefully. Those who have that gift can become great athletes. Those who don't, can't—no matter how hard they train. Many boys have that gift, but it is given to few girls—or at least few of them do anything with it."

Donna thought about what her father was saying, not understanding all of it.

"That's all I have to say to you," he continued. "We will stop the diving lessons for now. But think about that gift I told you about. You'll only be able to use it while you are young. It would be a shame to waste it."

He turned out the light on the table beside her bed and tucked the blanket around her shoulders. Kissing her on the forehead, he said, "Good night, honey."

"Good night, Daddy," she said in a solemn voice.

In the darkness she thought once more about standing on the ten-foot board and gazing down at the water far below, and she began to tremble. Then she remembered her father's words: "You don't have to dive if you don't want to. . . ." and felt warm and safe again.

Now she remembered what her father had said about a certain gift. That excited her. Nothing gave her more pleasure than to hit a home run or to kick a football farther than any of her brother's friends could. Nothing upset her more than to be only bat girl on the Little League team when she could play as well as most of the boys.

Sports seemed to belong to the boys. Yet there were some things a girl could do. Not diving. But what about swimming? She liked to swim, even though she had never seriously trained for it.

"Yes, I will think about swimming," she told herself as she slowly drifted off to sleep.

CHAPTER 2

BACK TO SAN FRANCISCO

Donna sat down at the kitchen table—and stared at the meal before her.

"This is breakfast?" she asked as her father entered the kitchen.

"Sure—an athlete's breakfast!" he told her. "Lamb chop, baked potato, Jell-o, tea—plenty of good food for your muscles. It will give you energy without slowing you down."

"If you say so," Donna agreed, picking up her fork. Her father knew a good athlete's breakfast if anyone did. Hadn't he been a big professional football star before he went into the insurance business?

And it was important, now, that Donna treat herself like an athlete. Almost a year had gone by since the night when the idea of swimming had entered her mind, and she had been doing something about it. During the past months she had spent a great deal of time working out, training as hard as she could.

She showed plenty of promise. The only trouble was,

there was no swimming coach available for youngsters her age in Lafayette. Frank McGuigan coached only divers, and although he assured her that she was a natural swimmer who had the qualities to be a winner, he couldn't train her.

As often as he could, Mr. deVarona helped her, but he was the first to admit that he was no professional swimming coach. Donna had entered some local swimming races, and she had won them. But again, those weren't professionals she was swimming against —they were simply other girls like herself.

Today, though—this would be different. Today would tell the story, Donna thought, as she made herself put away the huge breakfast. Today she was entered in a real, honest-to-goodness swimming meet. Not just here in Lafayette, but in San Francisco!

It was 7 o'clock when Mr. deVarona suggested that it was time to leave for San Francisco. Donna kissed her mother and carried the traveling bag to the car. As the car backed out of the drive, her brother and sister came out of the house and waved.

Mr. deVarona swung the car on to the highway that would lead through the East Bay towns and across the Bay Bridge to San Francisco. During the drive, Donna had time to think about the adventure that lay ahead.

It was her first Amateur Athletic Union Swimming Meet, and she was just beginning to understand what it meant. The Amateur Athletic Union, called the AAU, held meets for the best young swimmers, and this one was called the Far Western Meet. Girls from all over the western part of the United States—even Hawaii—would be in competition against each other.

"We are almost there," Mr. deVarona said.

They had driven through downtown San Francisco and into the green strip of land that was Golden Gate Park. Donna saw familiar sights—the meadows filled with sheep, the lakes with ducks and swans skimming over them. She could still remember back to the time when she was six and her family used to come to the park for Sunday picnics.

She remembered Fleischacker Pool, too. To a girl of six it had seemed as big as a lake. She had taken the first swims she could remember at Fleischacker, with her father at her side. And now she was going to compete there!

It was even bigger than Donna remembered, and her heart sank as she looked at it. The pool was so big that life guards were patrolling it in rowboats.

"Do I have to swim all that way?" Donna asked.

"Oh, no," Mr. deVarona said. "There's a marker tape in the water where you are supposed to stop. The course in only fifty yards."

That didn't help Donna. Everything looked grim. She and her father had left the early morning sunshine of Lafayette to enter gray San Francisco—foggy as always. The dull sky didn't help Donna's spirits, nor did the appearance of the pool water, which was green and cloudy.

And cold. Donna decided to jump into the pool for a trial work-out, and she came out shivering.

"Don't they heat that water?" she asked an older girl who was standing near her.

"Oh, sure," said the girl. "I think they use a candle. Maybe someone blew it out."

Mr. deVarona got out the old sleeping bag he had brought along, and Donna curled up inside it as they watched the meet begin.

The sight of her fellow swimmers did not raise Donna's spirits either. There were hundreds of girls around the pool, and she noticed that many of them wore suits with emblems of the organizations they belonged to—the Santa Clara Swimming Club, the Berkeley YMCA, the Los Angeles Athletic Club, the Multnomah Club from Portland, two clubs from Honolulu. Those girls seemed to know exactly what to do. They engaged in exercises before the start of their races. They had conferences with their coaches. They all seemed full of confidence—and Donna had anything but that. "It is like being in a foreign country," she thought. "I don't know any of the customs—I hardly can speak the language!"

She and her father sat beside the pool waiting—and waiting. Heat after heat (as the first races were called) was run off but Donna's event wasn't called.

As she watched the older swimmers perform, she grew more discouraged.

"I don't think I have a chance against them," she told her father. "They know so much more than I do."

"Don't worry about it, honey," her father said. "Just go in there and do your best. That's all that anybody expects of you."

The afternoon wore on, and Donna was beset with another concern—hunger. She hadn't eaten anything since her athlete's breakfast early that morning. Her stomach felt empty, yet she knew the danger of taking any food. Her race might be called at any minute.

Finally, at 5 P.M., her heat was announced. Donna slipped off her sweat shirt and walked toward the starting boxes at the edge of the pool. Eight other girls took places on either side of her.

"Who is that girl in lane number five?" inquired a loud voice.

Donna looked to both sides to see what was wrong. She noticed that the lane on her left was numbered four and the lane on her right was six.

At the side of the pool was a big, jolly-looking man, who was staring directly at her. She raised her hand.

"And just who are you, number five?" he asked.

"Donna deVarona from Lafayette," she said weakly.

"Well, Miss deVarona," the starter replied, "it is always helpful if you report to the judges before the race. That way, we will know who you are if you happen to win."

Donna felt her face burn. How awful—everyone was looking at her! She hadn't known that all swimmers were required to give their names to the judges before the race. When she had appeared in meets at home in Lafayette, she had just walked to the starting position, ready to swim.

"Swimmers, take your marks!" announced the starter, and he stood with gun in hand for the beginning of the race. Donna stepped on the box at the side of the pool and stood ready to dive in. But the girl in the lane next to her leaned too far forward and fell into the water before the gun sounded. The other swimmers waited as the girl climbed out of the pool and took her position again.

"Swimmers, take your marks!"

This time the girl in the number eight lane fell into the water before the race could begin. Then it happened to the number six girl, and Donna grew more and more nervous about the start. She was surprised when the starter walked over to her.

"Number five," he said, "it would help if you would bend down like the rest of the girls when I say, 'Swimmers, take your marks.' You have them all confused when you stand up the way you do, and they don't know whether to start or not."

Once again Donna turned a deep red. She had never

learned to assume the position for the racing dive—
she just dived into the water the way she usually
would.

"Swimmers, take your marks!"

This time Donna looked at the other swimmers and
bent down the way they did for the start. Finally
the race began. Donna had dived into the water and
taken two strokes when she heard another crack of the
gun, which meant that one of the swimmers had
started too early. That swimmer, she soon found out,
was number five, Donna deVarona!

On the next start, Donna thought, "This time was
all right—we are finally off!" Yet when she was half
way down the course she felt a rope in her way. It
was a special bar to stop swimmers who didn't hear
the second gun shot that meant a false start.

Donna could scarcely swim back to the starting
position, so great were her shame and anger with herself. She expected the starter to bawl her out—"And
he'd have every right!" she thought unhappily. But
to her surprise, he came over and put his big arm
around her.

"I think you are a little too eager, number five,"
he said. "And probably a little tired after all that
jumping into the water. Tell you what we will do.
We will let you girls rest for a while and take your
heat later."

It wasn't until 7 o'clock in the evening that Donna's

race was called once more. She still had eaten nothing since breakfast, and she was weak from hunger and anxious after the long wait. But win or lose, she made up her mind to follow her father's instructions: to do her best. And she was equally sure she was not going to make a false start again.

She didn't. She got off to a fast start along with the other swimmers, and she swam with all the strength she had left. When she reached the finish, she looked up and saw a judge standing over her.

"You are second, young lady," he told her.

Donna was excited when she came out of the pool. "Does that mean I made the finals tomorrow?" she asked her father.

"I don't know," he said. "You placed number ten in all the heats, but there are only nine lanes in the pool."

The judges went into conference and brought forth their decision: Miss deVarona of Lafayette, California, would be allowed to swim in the finals, occupying the outside lane.

Donna leaped with joy. Even without training and without a swimming club behind her, she had managed to be the tenth fastest swimmer in her event.

Mr. deVarona had promised Donna that if she did make the finals they would stay for the night at the San Francisco home of the Stone family, who were close friends. Two of the Stone sons were swimmers, and

Donna had great fun with them that evening, playing darts and talking about the Far Western Meet.

"I want to win tomorrow," said Donna. "Oh, I'd just love to win!"

Jack Stone, who was an excellent swimmer himself, encouraged her hopes. The following morning, he presented her with a small bowl that contained a live goldfish.

"It's for you," he announced, "to remind you to swim like a fish."

Donna was convinced that it would bring her good luck, and she threw her arms around Jack to thank him.

She was full of confidence when she and her father reported to Fleischacker Pool the next morning. This time she had made up her mind not to make the foolish mistakes she had made before. "Today is a new day," she told her father, "and today I'm going to be right all the way."

Once again she was forced to wait all through the morning and into the afternoon. Finally, at 4 o'clock, her race was called. Donna advanced to the starting box, taking her position at the end of the row, tenth in line. The starter noticed her and said, "Now *please* wait until I shoot off the gun!"

"Don't worry," Donna assured him.

"Swimmers, take your marks!"

Donna and the other nine girls advanced to the

edge of the pool and stood on their boxes. Donna bent down when the others did, waiting for the starter's signal. The gun sounded and she dived toward the water. It was a perfect start, ten young bodies splashing the surface at the same time.

Her arms working swiftly, Donna churned through the water as fast as she could. But there was no line on the bottom of the pool for her to follow, and several times she bumped against the cable that separated the lanes. She was bruised each time, but she kept swimming.

She reached the narrow marker at the end of the course, but it was only a narrow strip. There was no surface for her to push off from, as on the end of a pool. Donna turned around as quickly as possible and began her return to the other end of the pool.

She finished with a burst of energy and looked up quickly, but there was no judge to tell her how she had finished. She climbed out of the pool and saw her father advancing with a towel.

"How did I do?" she asked eagerly.

"You finished tenth, Liz," he told her.

Suddenly the strain of the two days of competition was too much for her. She broke into tears. Mr. deVarona put his arm around her shoulder and said softly, "Now, honey, don't be upset because you lost. You did well to take part in the finals."

"I'm not crying because I lost," she answered. "It's

just—well, I might have *won* if I had had enough training."

"Yes, you might have," her father agreed. "And next time I hope you'll have it."

CHAPTER 3

"A GOOD NATURAL
SWIMMER"

Donna followed her father up the path to the club house of the Berkeley Women's Club. She recognized the emblem outside the building as one she had seen on the suits of swimmers she raced against in the Far Western Meet at Fleischacker Pool. The Berkeley Women's Club, her father had discovered, had a swimming club for young girls, and it might offer a place where Donna could get her training.

"But Berkeley is a long way from our house," Donna pointed out. "How could I get there?"

"Don't worry about that," Mr. deVarona answered. "We will work it out somehow."

Donna and her father entered the club house and went to the office of Lorabelle Brooksaver, who was in charge of the club's swimming program.

"Oh, yes, Mr. deVarona," said the short, friendly woman. "I remember your daughter from the Far Western Meet."

34

Donna blushed, thinking of the false starts she had made. But the coach didn't mention them.

"I was impressed with Donna at the meet," Miss Brooksaver went on. "She certainly showed she had a lot of fight."

"Yes, she's a serious girl," Mr. deVarona said. "And I think she can be an excellent swimmer. But we know that natural ability itself is not enough. We don't have training facilities and expert coaching in Lafayette so I thought that perhaps she could enroll in your program here."

Donna dressed in her swim suit and reported to the pool. Miss Brooksaver instructed her to swim the free style, back stroke, breast stroke and butterfly, the four strokes that competition swimmers use in races. Donna swam two laps of each. Then she was told to dry off and get dressed, while her father talked with Miss Brooksaver in the office.

"Yes, Donna is as I remember her at Fleischacker— a good natural swimmer," the coach said. "But, as you have pointed out, she has not had the training that would be necessary for her to swim in competition."

"What would you suggest?" Mr. deVarona asked.

"Donna needs instruction in all four strokes," was the answer. "That would mean private coaching before she could begin swimming with the team." She outlined the cost and what Donna's part in the club's program would mean.

On the drive back to Lafayette, Mr. deVarona told Donna, "I'm afraid you won't be able to take coaching there. I wish you could, but it's just too expensive. We can't afford it right now. Besides, your mother would have to join the mother's club, and she just wouldn't be able to spare the time away from home."

Donna was very disappointed. But she wouldn't let herself beg or tease. So much of her family's time—yes, and money, too—was already taken up by her swimming. And yet . . . well, "How am I ever going to get to be a real swimmer without training?" she thought. Her father would know a way out.

Mr. deVarona himself worked with Donna at an Oakland pool until he thought she was ready to try another meet. He chose the Novice Meet, which the Berkeley YMCA conducted for those who had never won a medal in a swimming meet before.

"Do you think I'm ready for it, Dad?" Donna asked.

"I think so," her father answered. "You'll be swimming 25-yard races only. That means your condition won't matter so much. It's your speed that will count."

And he was right. Donna won the free style and back stroke races with excellent times for a girl her age.

As Donna and her father were leaving the YMCA after the meet, they were approached by a tall, broadly built man.

"You this girl's father?" the man asked.

"Yes, I'm Dave deVarona," Mr. deVarona answered.

"My name's Swenson; I'm coach of the Berkeley Y team," the man announced. "I think this girl has possibilities. I'd be willing to take her in one of our classes. You interested?"

"Yes, I am," Mr. deVarona said, "if you could tell me what the conditions would be."

"A small charge for a locker and use of the pool. Hour-and-a-half classes every day, Saturday and Sunday included."

Donna's father turned to her. "Would you like to, Liz?" he asked.

"Oh, yes!" she replied.

"Well, I'd like her to try it," Mr. deVarona told the coach. "Only trouble is, we live in Lafayette, and I'm not sure how we would get her here every day."

"That can be arranged. We have other girls from Lafayette; she can join a car pool."

With this last problem out of the way, it was quickly settled that Donna would start the next Monday at 5:30.

Donna was in a state of high excitement as she arrived at the Berkeley YMCA for her first practice. She had been chatting with the other girls in the car coming from Lafayette, and she was still talking as she followed them into the locker room. Then she noticed that all of them fell silent.

"What's the matter?" Donna asked.

"Mr. Swenson doesn't allow any talking in the locker room," whispered one of the girls.

"What a silly rule!" Donna said. "Why can't we talk?"

"Don't ask why," the girl answered. "Just follow directions."

"Is Mr. Swenson going to be our coach?" Donna asked, dropping her voice to a whisper.

"No, he's away right now," said the girl. "Anyway, he coaches the senior team and you will be on the junior team."

"If he's away, why do we have to whisper?" Donna asked.

"Shhhh!" The girl glanced down the hall as if she expected "Swede" Swenson to appear.

Donna still didn't understand the rule, but she undressed in silence and put on her new swimming suit. She looked in the full-length mirror and admired the emblem that indicated she was now a member of the Berkeley YMCA swimming team.

"All right, girls! On the double!" shouted a man's voice from outside the dressing room. "Time to go to work!"

Donna joined the other girls in hurrying out to the pool area. There she saw a tall man in gray slacks and white T-shirt, with a whistle hanging from a string around his neck.

"You the new kid?" he asked.

"Yes, sir," she replied. "I'm Donna deVarona."

"Oh, yes, I've heard about you. I'm Jack Barkely, and I'm going to be your coach. First of all, we are going to see what you can do."

For the next half hour Donna joined the other girls in swimming laps back and forth in the pool. Toward the end, Donna thought her lungs would burst or her arms would fall off, or both. Finally she heard the whistle blow and the coach shout, "Take two."

Donna saw the other girls head for the end of the pool, and she followed them. She asked a girl named Linda, "What does he mean—'take two?'"

"Take two minutes' rest, of course," Linda answered.

"Two minutes! Is that all we get?" Donna dragged herself out of the water and lay panting on the deck.

Linda laughed, "Oh, you'll get used to this pace, if it doesn't kill you first. Maybe some day you'll be able to swim the whole hour and a half without resting, like Carol Swenson."

"Who's she?"

Linda stared at her in surprise. "You mean you don't know who Carol Swenson is?"

"No. Should I?"

"She only holds the record in the 400, that's all."

"Is she related to Swede Swenson?" Donna asked.

"Of course. She's his daughter. Both Carol and her

younger sister Jan swim for the Berkeley Y. That's Carol over there."

Donna gazed at the girl swimming in the deep end. "Boy, she looks good all right," said Donna. "No wonder she holds the record!"

The shrill sound of the whistle summoned Donna and the other members of the junior team back into the pool, and the laps continued. At the end of the hour and a half, Donna could hardly summon the strength to return to the locker room and change back into her clothes. As she walked outside, she met Coach Barkely.

"Tired, Donna?" he asked.

"Yes, sir," she admitted.

"I think you'll be able to sleep tonight." He smiled. "In fact, you'll probably begin in the car on the drive back to Lafayette. Well, you are not afraid of hard work, are you?"

"No, sir."

"Good! Because you'll get plenty of it if you stay at the Berkeley Y. Swimming is ten per cent natural ability and ninety per cent work. I think you have the natural ability. We will see if you are able to take the work. The main thing is not to become discouraged if you don't start winning races right away. Most girls swim a year or two before they start placing at meets. Some girls never do place. But even though there's fun in winning, it's a fine experience to be part of a team. Don't you think so, Donna?"

"Yes, sir. I'm sure I'm going to like it," she told him, and it was true, even though she was so tired.

"I will get used to it," she thought. "It may take a while, but I will get used to it."

"Just to give you something to aim for," the coach went on, "I think I will have you enter some ten-year-old races in an Amateur Athletic Union meet at Alameda Air Station in about three weeks. I don't expect you to perform any miracle. But I think the competition will be good experience for you."

It was at the Alameda meet that Donna first met Debbie Lee. She was a bright-eyed girl a few months older than Donna and with much more experience in competition. Donna met her as they were waiting for the start of the races at the naval air station.

"Say—were you in the races at the Far Western Meet at Fleischacker Pool last August?" Debbie asked.

"Yes, I'm the one who made all the false starts," Donna confessed. "I don't think I will ever live that down."

"Oh, I wouldn't worry about that," Debbie said. "You made the finals, didn't you?"

"Uh-huh," Donna said—not adding that she had scored tenth out of ten swimmers.

"What are you swimming today?"

41

"The coach has me entered in the 50-yard races—all of them," said Donna.

"Well, I wish you luck," Debbie said.

"Thank you. Same to you."

At first it looked as though Donna's luck had been left at home. She got off to a good start in the breast stroke, but her style was so odd that she was put out of the race. The same thing happened in the butterfly.

"That's all right," Coach Barkely said. "Now you know the work you have to do on your strokes."

But Donna wasn't ready to give up on the meet and charge it all up to experience. As she waited for the free style race to begin, she told herself, "I'll make up for those two races this time!"

She did. When the race was over, Coach Barkely and her fellow members of the Berkeley YMCA team were surprised to find that Donna deVarona had finished third.

Next she came up against her new friend, Debbie Lee, in the back stroke. Debbie had won the Far Western race in which Donna had finished a poor last. This time Donna got off to a fast start. While Debbie took the lead immediately, Donna was not far behind, and she finished only three-tenths of a second behind Debbie.

Cheers went up from the members of the Berkeley YMCA. Coach Barkely ran up to hug Donna and exclaim, "I never thought you'd do it! I absolutely never thought you'd do it!"

Donna couldn't reply. Her heart was in her throat —and not because she was tired from four fast races. It was the thrill of having come so close to victory that made her so excited.

So close—but not close enough. That would come later, she vowed.

CHAPTER 4

COACH SWENSON

Donna continued to score well in swimming meets, although she still was unable to achieve her goal of winning a race. The prospect of winning a medal was enough to keep her going, and she continued her daily work-outs at the Berkeley YMCA, pushing herself a little harder each day.

At the end of one long practice, she pulled herself out of the pool and found herself faced with the huge form of Swede Swenson. The coach, who had just returned to the Y, stared down at Donna.

"You call that a work-out?" he demanded. "Why, my daughters were swimming that hard when they were seven years old. And that back stroke! Why do you have to put your arms way out in the water? Why can't you keep them close to your body and save all that energy?"

Donna practiced her back stroke, keeping her arms close to her sides.

44

"Of course!" he said. "You don't have to flap through the water like a windmill. You'll have to do better than that when you swim for me."

Donna stared at him, not believing what she heard. "When I swim for you?" she asked.

"Right," he answered firmly. "I'm taking over your coaching."

He departed, leaving Donna in a state of joy and wonder. She could hardly wait to get home and tell her father and mother the news. She would be swimming with the best competition in the Berkeley YMCA, not just the girls who were ten and eleven years old. But along with her delight was a feeling of concern.

Now she would be swimming with the best. Even though she had been receiving expert coaching for less than a year, she would be expected to maintain the same pace as girls who had been training very hard for six, seven, or eight years. She knew that Coach Swenson would grant her no special favors because of her age and size. It would be up to her to produce results—or get out.

A chilly fog hung over Berkeley on the day Donna reported for her first practice with her new coach.

"All right, girls," Coach Swenson announced after they had assembled, "three times around the park."

As the girls started toward the door, Donna asked her friend Linda, "What does he mean?"

"He means we are going to run around the park three times," said Linda.

Donna managed to tag along with the others as they raced through the park. When they reported back to the YMCA, the coach directed them into the gymnasium.

"What now?" Donna asked.

"We lift weights and do exercises," Linda explained.

"When do we swim?" said Donna.

"Oh, you'll get enough swimming," Linda said quickly.

Donna soon found out what Linda meant. When the work-out was over, she was too tired to follow the other girls into the locker room. She had to sit down on a bench and recover her strength.

"Too much for you?" asked Coach Swenson.

Breathing too deeply to speak, Donna shook her head.

"You have so much to learn!" the coach said in despair. "I don't know if it is worth the trouble. For instance, why do you take a breath after every stroke of the butterfly? You don't need that air. You just tire yourself out by breathing so rapidly. Your stroke will be smoother if you breathe every second stroke. Another thing. What side do you breathe on in the free style?"

Donna had to practice her stroke so she could remember. "On the right side," she replied.

"Why?"

"I don't know. I guess because I'm right-handed."

"That's no reason. If you keep breathing on the right side, you're going to favor your right stroke. Then your free style will not be even. Breathe on both sides, first the right, then the left, then the right again. Your stroke will be more balanced."

"Yes, sir," Donna answered.

She began to shiver. She felt cold, now that she was sitting still. The coach shook his head. "How much do you weigh?" he demanded.

"Sixty-five pounds," she said.

"Sixty-five pounds!" he exclaimed. "How can I make a swimmer out of a runt who weighs sixty-five pounds! Tell your mother to give you pills to put some fat on you so I can make something out of you."

Donna went into the locker room and gazed at Carol and Jan Swenson. They were five feet eight or nine inches—more than a foot taller than Donna—and she guessed that they must weigh close to one hundred and fifty pounds.

"I will never be that big," Donna thought, "and I don't want to be. Who says you have to be big and full of muscles to become a champion swimmer?"

That was just one of the things she wanted to prove the coach wrong about.

47

The morning was bright and cheerful, and Donna was happy. She and her father were driving east on the highway to Fresno, on their way to Donna's first meet as an eleven-year-old. Donna's birthday, a few days before, had been an important event. It allowed her to graduate from the ten-years-and-younger class— which now seemed terribly young to her.

"Today," she thought, as the countryside slipped past the car windows, "I will be in competition with the big girls. Why, some of them have been swimming in the eleven-to-twelve group for almost two years!"

She looked out the window, feeling warm and good inside. "You're kind of quiet, honey," her father said, after a while.

"I've been thinking," Donna told him. "I'm going to show them that a skinny little 'runt' can keep right up with them, and maybe pull ahead and win."

Donna didn't say so, but the Fresno meet would place her in competition with Jan Swenson for the first time. That pleased her. For weeks, she had set her sights on Jan Swenson as her first big challenge in the eleven-to-twelve age group. Jan was the queen of the twelve-year-olds at the Berkeley YMCA, she held many of the national records in her age class, and she was looked up to by most of the younger swimmers.

Donna didn't look up to Jan Swenson, she looked *at* her. She studied the older, heavier swimmer, the good and weak elements of her stroke. Could she ever

48

beat the coach's daughter in a race? No stranger would have given Donna a chance—although she had gained an inch in height and ten pounds in weight, she still was almost a foot shorter than Jan and half as heavy. But anyone who knew Donna wouldn't have bet against her—that deVarona girl was a very determined little person.

"What are you thinking about now?" her father asked as they passed through another small farm town.

"The meet," Donna said.

"Maybe you should try to catch a little nap," he suggested. "It would be good for you."

"Oh, I couldn't sleep now. I'm much too excited."

"Well, I hope you didn't forget anything in your excitement. Did you bring your hair brush and an extra dress?"

"Yes, I'm sure I did."

"Sure, are you? The state you are in, I wouldn't be surprised if you left your swim suit behind."

"Oh!" Donna gasped.

"What is it?" her father asked.

"I don't remember packing my swim suit!"

Mr. deVarona looked at her, stopped the car, and walked around to the trunk. He looked in Donna's bag and found no suit.

There was nothing to be done about it. As they went on, Donna asked in a worried voice, "What will I do?

Mr. Swenson will kill me if I don't have a Berkeley Y suit."

"Mr. Swenson is not going to kill you over a small matter like that," her father said. "We will buy a new one."

"But it is Sunday and the stores are closed!"

"Don't worry, Donna. We will think of something."

When Mr. deVarona drove up before the stadium at Fresno, Donna spotted a familiar face. "Stop the car, please, Dad," she said. "There's someone I want to see."

Leaping out of the car, she called "Debbie Lee! Wait!" and raced after her friend, who was entering the locker rooms.

Debbie turned around and smiled a welcome. "Hi! Are you swimming today?"

"Yes, but I may have to do it in my birthday suit," said Donna. "I left my Berkeley Y suit at home."

"I could lend you one of mine," Debbie offered. "We are about the same size, and I have a spare."

"Gee, that would be great!" Donna said.

"There's only one trouble," Debbie added, as she looked through her traveling bag.

"What's that?"

Debbie pulled out the spare suit and pointed at the emblem of the Santa Clara Swim Club.

"Oh, I don't mind wearing your club's emblem,"

said Donna. "And I promise not to disgrace Santa Clara. Thanks a lot, Debbie. I will get it back to you after the meet is over." Donna raced back to the car with the suit in hand.

When she appeared on the deck for her work-out, she came face to face with Coach Swenson. There was a look of horror on his face.

"What is *that?*" he demanded.

"What?" Donna asked. In her excitement, she had forgotten about the borrowed suit.

"What is that suit you are wearing?" the coach asked, his face growing red.

"Oh, this!" Donna said brightly. "Well, you see, I forgot to pack my own suit. I didn't think about it until I was half way here with Dad, and then it was too late to turn back and get it. Anyway, I couldn't very well swim without any suit at all—they just don't allow that. So I borrowed a suit from a friend."

"You borrowed a Santa Clara suit?" The coach seemed all the more surprised because Donna seemed to see nothing wrong in what she had done.

"Yes, I know this girl, Debbie Lee. You know her— a pretty blond girl; she beat me at the Alameda meet in the 50-yard back stroke."

"She's a friend of yours?"

"Yes. We talk a lot before meets."

"You listen to me, Donna deVarona!" the coach said.

"As long as you are a member of my team, you do *not* make friends with swimmers of the other teams. You stay with members of the Berkeley Y only. Is that understood?"

"Yes, sir," said Donna, crossing her fingers behind her back.

"And you are not going to race for me while you wear the suit of another club," he continued. "Go back to the locker room and take it off."

"But I can't do that, coach," Donna replied. "I don't have another suit. And besides, I'm due in the water now for my warm-up." With that she dived into the water, leaving her coach talking to himself.

Donna gathered with the other eleven-year-olds for the final event of the day, the 100-yard free style. All the others were doing the "swimmer's shake," shaking their arms to ease their nervous feelings and speed the circulation of their blood. But Donna wasn't nervous. She stood quietly, watching big Jan Swenson, who would be one of the swimmers in the race.

"Hey, that suit looks good on you!"

Donna turned to see Debbie Lee admiring the Santa Clara suit.

"Yes, it is a good fit," Donna replied.

"I mean the 'Santa Clara' on the suit," Debbie said, with a grin. "That's what looks good on you."

"Swimmers, take your marks!" The starter's signal brought the half-dozen girls to the starting boxes, and now Donna felt the rush of excitement that always came before a race. Then there was no more time to think. The race was beginning.

Donna got off to a good start, as did the other swimmers. All six remained bunched together until the first turn, and then Debbie Lee pushed out in front. Jan Swenson was not far behind her, and then came Donna and three other girls.

The second turn found Debbie and Jan farther out in front, but now Donna had pulled away from the three girls who had been beside her. She was beginning to close the gap between herself and Jan.

After the third turn, Donna told herself, "It is now or never." She exploded with a burst of speed and didn't let down until she felt the edge of the pool under her hand. The other girls were finishing around her, and she was too tired to do anything more than hang on to the side and gasp for air.

As the noise of the crowd died down, she heard a voice over the loud speaker: "Winner of the eleven-year-old 100 free style: Debbie Lee, Santa Clara. Second: Donna deVarona, Berkeley YMCA. Third: Jan Swenson, Berkeley YMCA."

Donna could scarcely believe her ears. She climbed out of the pool and saw her father approaching.

"Oh, Dad, I did it!" she exclaimed, throwing her arms around him and completely soaking his clothes.

She repeated it to herself, almost unable to believe it. "I did it! I beat Jan Swenson. I hoped to do it some day—but I beat her today!"

CHAPTER 5

"I'VE GOT TO
PROVE MYSELF"

"Happy birthday to you; happy birthday to you; happy birthday, dear Daddy; happy birthday to you."

David deVarona blinked open his eyes and saw a lovely sight: Deet, Donna, and Joanne smiling down at him from the end of the bed. His wife Martha was standing behind them, holding the newest addition to the family, baby Kurt.

"Good heavens, it *is* my birthday," Mr. deVarona said, sitting up in bed. "I'm getting to be an old man."

"Oh, you are not so old," said Deet. He spoke from experience. His father could keep up with him in the rough work-outs he took in the back yard to prepare for the high school football season.

"This is what you get for being a good daddy," said Donna as she placed a breakfast tray on her father's lap.

"Breakfast in bed!" he said. "Wait until I tell them about this at the office!"

"And this is something from me," said Joanne, handing him an envelope. Inside was a special birthday card that she had drawn and decorated with crayons.

"Thank you, dear," said Mr. deVarona, "and thank you all. Since you've been so kind, I'm going to do something for you. Tonight I'm going to quit work early and we will all go to San Francisco and have dinner in Chinatown. All except you, Kurt. I'm afraid you'll have to stay home with a baby sitter."

"All right, children, better finish your breakfasts," said Mrs. deVarona. "You'll be late for school if you don't."

She put Kurt down in his crib with the morning bottle and went to the kitchen. She found Deet and Joanne talking away, excited about the trip to San Francisco. But Donna was strangely quiet.

"More oatmeal, Donna?" her mother asked.

"No, thank you," Donna replied.

"Why so sad? Aren't you excited about going to Chinatown for dinner?"

"I can't go," Donna said.

"Can't go? Why not?"

"Because I have swimming practice." Donna got up and ran to her room, tears in her eyes.

Mrs. deVarona was distressed, and she went into the bedroom to talk to her husband. "Honestly, Dave!" she said. "Donna thinks she can't go to dinner with us because she has swimming practice. There's no reason why she can't take part in family activities. She is simply too wrapped up in her swimming, not thinking of anything else. It is not right. She should be able to enjoy the normal things that other girls her age do."

"I agree. That's why I told her she couldn't work out on Fridays, when kids are supposed to have fun. But you can't say that swimming hasn't been good for her. She has done much better in her school work since she started training. She has made many new friends, while once she didn't have many friends at all. And she has been able to keep up in her Girl Scout troop and her art classes after school."

"Yes, I know, Dave, and I'm proud of what she has done. But tonight's your birthday!"

"Let me talk to her, Marty. I agree—she could afford to miss one night's practice."

Mr. deVarona dressed and went to Donna's room, where she was assembling her books to take to school.

"Don't you think Swede Swenson could spare you just once, so you could help me celebrate my birthday?" he asked.

"I can't miss practice, Dad," Donna insisted. "He gets awfully mad if I do. He says I'm chicken."

"I don't care what the coach says, and you shouldn't have to, either. I'm getting fed up. If I could find another good club for you to join, I'd take you out of the Berkeley Y."

"But I don't want to leave it," Donna protested. "I've got to prove myself."

"Then you must just take the good that he has to offer as a coach and not let him upset you."

"I will try, Dad."

"Are you sure you don't want to ride the cable car with us tonight?"

"I want to—but I have to practice."

He gave her a hug. "I understand. I was the same way about football many birthdays ago. I gave up a lot of the fun that other boys had; it was more important to me to practice. I will tell you this—I never regretted my choice, and I don't think you will, either."

When the 2 o'clock bell rang at school that afternoon, Donna hurried to her locker and took out her heavy jacket. Even though the sun was shining brightly in Lafayette, it would be windy and cold when she got home that night. She picked out books for the three subjects in which she had homework and tucked them under her arm, along with her notebook. She glanced at her watch and started running. The bus to Berkeley was loading by the time she arrived.

As she had expected, the weather was gray and damp when she stepped off the bus in Berkeley. She buttoned up her jacket and began the mile walk to the Swenson house.

The door was not locked. Ever since practice had been shifted from the Berkeley YMCA to the bigger pool on Treasure Island, Donna had been reporting each afternoon to the Swenson's house. She would wait there for an hour until Mr. and Mrs. Swenson had picked up their daughters at school, and then they would drive Donna and other swimmers across the bay to Treasure Island.

Donna had been working on her English during the bus ride, and she sat down on the living room couch to continue the homework. After half an hour, she grew restless. She closed her notebook and started pacing about the house, thinking about the work-out. She wandered into the den.

She had never been in that room before, and she was surprised by the display. All around the den, in bookcases and on a rail near the ceiling, were cups, plates, and statues of swimmers, all in gleaming silver and brass. Nearly all of them had been won by Carol Swenson, and many were the top prizes in swimming competition. Donna examined every one.

"What are you doing?"

The voice broke the quiet of the house, and Donna started. She turned around to see Mrs. Swenson, a tall woman with broad shoulders, staring down at her.

"Oh, I was just looking at Carol's prizes," Donna explained. "She sure has a lot of them."

"Come on. We are leaving," was all Mrs. Swenson said.

The drive to Treasure Island was a silent one, as it always was. Mr. and Mrs. Swenson sat in the front seat with Carol between them. Jan was in the second seat with two other girls. Donna and three girls sat in the flat area between the second seat and the tail gate.

The station wagon swung out of the trail of traffic at Yerba Buena Island and headed down the road to Treasure Island, the man-made piece of land built for a world's fair and later used by the navy.

The girls put on their swim suits quickly—and silently—and reported to the huge indoor pool, where the Berkeley YMCA was allowed two lanes. That meant that they had to swim in a line, up one lane and down the other, the fastest swimmers in front. Carol Swenson was first, of course. Donna would have been entitled to swim behind her—except that Mrs. Swenson was now working out with the team, and she swam behind her oldest daughter.

The swimming practice was the same as it always was. First came fifty meters of back stroke, breast stroke, butterfly, and free style. Then came twelve laps of kicking, without use of hands and arms. Then twelve laps of arm strokes, without kicking. Just to make sure that nobody kicked, the coach made each swimmer fasten a rubber band around her ankles. Once when she was especially weary, Donna had taken off the band, and Coach Swenson had found it in the pool gutter. After the scolding he gave her, she vowed never to disobey his instructions again.

"All right, I want six laps by each of you, with the girl behind you holding on to your legs," the coach announced.

When Donna had finished that, she was required to swim six laps with her head out of the water, then kick six laps the same way.

Finally the rest period came: two minutes on the deck—and then the girls were ordered back into the pool for four races of four hundred meters each. After another brief rest, the practice ended with the 400-meter individual.

Coach Swenson stood at the end of the pool with a stop watch in his hand, starting each girl at set intervals. He always announced the time for each one as she finished her laps.

He shouted Carol's time as she touched the edge of the pool. But when Donna finished, he just shook the watch, as if he didn't believe what he saw. Finally he put it away in his pocket.

On the drive home that night, Coach Swenson broke his usual silence to speak to Carol. He seemed to feel that she might not have put forth her best in the work-out. Was she becoming careless in her strokes? Carol tried to deny it but was told to be silent.

"What was my time?" Donna wondered to herself. "Why didn't he announce it? Was the watch broken?" The conversation between Carol and her father was putting a new idea into her head. Had her time, just possibly, been faster than Carol's? She could hardly believe it, but maybe, just maybe, that was it!

At the Swenson house Donna and another girl were picked up by the girl's father, a doctor who worked late in the city. He drove to Orinda and left Donna at a corner drug store, where she put a dime in the pay phone and called her home number. After two rings, she hung up; that was the signal for her father to come and get her. While she waited for him to drive the few miles from Lafayette, she bought herself a candy bar with the dime she had saved on the telephone call.

By the time she reached home, Kurt and Joanne were asleep and Deet was finishing his homework. It was 9:30, and Donna still had a book report to write for her English class. First, she sat down to the hot dinner that her mother had waiting for her.

"We missed you tonight," Mrs. deVarona said, sitting down at the kitchen table while Donna ate. "We rode the cable car up California Street and had a wonderful dinner at Johnny Kan's. I wish you could have been with us."

Her daughter's weary face disturbed her. "Are you very tired, dear?" she asked, after a moment.

Donna nodded. She ached in every muscle; even her bones seemed to ache.

"Oh, Donna, Donna!" her mother said. "Are you sure it's all worth it?"

Donna thought for a moment. "Yes, it's worth it," she said. Her aches felt good, for by now she was convinced that she had beaten Carol Swenson's time at Treasure Island that day.

CHAPTER 6

THE MILE SWIM

The sun was shining brightly as the big bus rumbled along the highway, and Donna's feelings matched the weather. It had not always been this way. There had been many gloomy days. Often she had made the trip to Berkeley with a heavy heart, feeling that she would rather spend the afternoon exploring the hills with her dog, or home exchanging hair styles with a friend or —well, doing almost anything in the world other than swimming.

But all that had changed. Lately, she found, she could hardly wait to make the long journey from Lafayette to Treasure Island. Donna had made an important discovery. It was one that comes sooner or later to all athletes, and the sooner it comes the better: *your only real competition is yourself*. Not the other swimmers. Your own self.

Now, when Donna put just a little more effort in the last lap of the 400 she was racing against her own time of the week before. There could be no off days with her. Each time she swam, she insisted that her performance be her best one. She kept pushing herself to the limit, and it surprised her to learn that she was always able to do more.

It had affected her in other ways, too. Her school work was improving. Partly because of the move from San Francisco to Lafayette, partly because Lafayette was growing and building new schools, Donna had attended five different schools in seven years, which left her more confused than confident. But now she was much more sure of herself, and her school work had improved. "Maybe," Donna thought, looking unseeingly out the bus window, "I am growing up."

"Here's your stop, miss," said the bus driver.

"Oh, my goodness, I must have been day dreaming," Donna exclaimed, grabbing her books and leaping out the door.

She ran for a block and a half, although it was difficult with an arm full of school books. Then she slowed down to a walk and continued toward the Swenson house, her heart beating fast from the run and from the excitement of the work-out ahead. Coach Swenson had been pushing the girls extra hard because of the nationals coming up soon at Redding, California. Donna didn't mind at all, but some of the swimmers complained to one another of being exhausted afterward. Donna never complained. She had learned to accept every challenge the coach put to her.

Donna turned the corner and walked faster as she approached the Swenson house. She thought she had a half hour to accomplish some homework before the Swensons arrived.

As she reached the house, she saw a piece of paper tacked to the door. It read:

"Donna—Couldn't wait for you—Karl N. Swenson."

She stared at the note. She couldn't believe that they had left without her. It had never happened before, because she had never been late. She glanced at her watch. It was still half an hour before the time when they always left for Treasure Island.

She knocked on the door and the noise echoed in the empty house. Confused and upset, Donna walked slowly back to the bus stop for the long ride home.

That night she telephoned the Swenson house.

"Coach, this is Donna," she began.

"Where were you this afternoon?" he wanted to know.

"I was at your house at the same time I always am."

"I told you practice would be an hour early today."

"You told me?" Donna tried to think back.

"Certainly. Last night after practice I told you and all the girls that I was quitting work early and we would go an hour earlier today. Weren't you listening?"

"I—I don't remember hearing it."

"I hope you can be on time tomorrow."

"I will be there, sir," Donna said quietly.

She hung up the phone and went to bed, blaming herself for not hearing the coach's instructions.

The following Friday, Coach Swenson reported on the practice meet that would be held in Richmond the next day. "All girls except Smith and deVarona will report to the Y at 8:30 in the morning," the coach said.

Donna asked Coach Swenson why she shouldn't report at the same time.

"Because you aren't going to be in the meet," he told her.

"Why not?" she asked.

"Because there isn't room for you in the car pool," he replied, walking away.

Donna was puzzled. She couldn't understand why the coach would leave her behind and take three other twelve-year-olds whose times were not as good as hers.

The more she thought about it, the more puzzled and upset she became. When her father picked her up at the drug store in Orinda, he found her in tears.

"What's the matter, Liz?" he asked.

"It is the coach," Donna said. "He won't take me to the nationals at Redding."

"Why not? Aren't you good enough?"

"Tonight I swam the 400 free style better than anyone except Carol Swenson."

"Then why won't he take you?"

"I don't know!" Donna said, the tears starting again.

"Well, we will see about that. I'm going to call him as soon as I get home!"

When they arrived home, David deVarona placed a telephone call to Berkeley.

"Why aren't you taking Donna to Redding?" he asked Coach Swenson.

"Because we don't have any more seats in the cars and we aren't able to get any more hotel rooms in Redding. There's a convention going on at the same time as the nationals," the coach explained.

"Then why don't you leave some of the other girls at home and take Donna?"

"Because she's not good enough."

"I think she is," Mr. deVarona said quietly. "I've seen her beat most of the other girls at practice."

"Are you questioning my judgment as coach?"

"No, I'm not," Mr. deVarona said. "But as father of one of the team members, I want to be sure she gets fair treatment."

"I will not have my decisions questioned! *I* am the coach of the Berkeley YMCA swimming team. What I say is final! Good night!"

Mr. deVarona hung up slowly. Then he said, "I will drive you up to Redding myself, Donna. I've got an old football buddy living there, so we won't have to worry about getting a hotel room. You'll swim in the nationals."

The next day at the Redding pool, Donna found Coach Swenson just as he was writing up the names of the Berkeley YMCA girls who would swim in the nationals. The crowd was beginning to fill up the stands beside the pool, and the first heats would be starting within the hour.

"Hi, coach," Donna said brightly. She enjoyed his surprised look. "My dad drove me up here," she added.

"I told him there were no more hotel rooms available," the coach said.

"No problem. A friend Dad used to play football with lives here in Redding. We are staying with him. Well, shall I take a warm-up swim?"

"Yes. Do that."

Donna walked to the edge of the pool. Other girls were beginning to work out, and she studied them. All of them looked much older and bigger. At twelve, Donna stood four feet ten inches and weighed only eighty-eight pounds. But she wasn't worried about her size. She knew that the only thing that mattered was who touched the finish line first.

She swam a dozen laps, stroking calmly and evenly. She was not going to let the excitement of swimming in the nationals upset her form. But she noticed that her heart was beating faster, and not from swimming the dozen laps.

Drying herself with a towel, Donna went to the card table where Coach Swenson was filling out the racing blanks.

"What am I going to swim, coach?" she asked. "I think I'd have the best chance in the free style. My times are getting better."

"Yes, I think I will have you swim the free style," the coach replied.

"Which one?"

"The 1760-yard."

Donna looked at him in surprise. It was the mile swim, a race she had never been in before.

"But I'm not ready for that," she protested.

"That's the only race where there is room for you today. Of course, if you'd rather not swim—"

"No, I will swim in it."

Donna knew she wouldn't have a chance in the mile swim. She would be up against older swimmers, including Carol Swenson, who had trained for years in distance swimming. But she made up her mind to do the best she could.

Donna finished tenth in the 1760-yard swim, a very fine record for a twelve-year-old who was racing against the best swimmers in the nation.

On the following days, Coach Swenson entered Donna in other difficult races—the 110-yard butterfly, the 220-yard butterfly. The competition in all of them was too tough. She didn't make any of the finals.

As she and her father drove back to Lafayette at the end of the meet, Donna was both excited and disappointed.

"We won!" she exclaimed to her father. "The Berkeley Y scored more points than any other team."

"You *should* feel proud," her father said, "even though you didn't do as well as you hoped. But it is your team, and you should take pride when it wins."

"That's just it, Dad," Donna said sadly. "I wish I could have helped the team more."

Her father shook his head. "You did all you could, Liz, and that's good enough for me."

CHAPTER 7

THE OLYMPICS

The year 1960 was an important one for Donna deVarona, as it was for the world's finest athletes. Once again the Olympic Games were to be held, this time in Rome, Italy. Thousands of men and women were in training with the hope of appearing in the world's greatest sporting event.

Not many people in the swimming world would have given Donna a chance to make the United States team. It was true that swimming champions were coming up younger as new training methods were bringing forth a new generation of speed marvels. But Donna would pass her thirteenth birthday only three months before the games were to be held. How could a girl so young race against full-grown swimmers?

It seemed quite possible to Donna. Now she was being trained by a new Berkeley YMCA coach, Tatto Yamashita, and his assistant, Jack Barkely, with whom she had worked before. Mr. Swenson had left to concentrate on coaching his daughters.

1. Donna deVarona's swimming career began in her home town of Lafayette, California. Her father, who had been a professional football star, was her coach. In her first AAU meet, she finished tenth—after many false starts—in a field of 10 swimmers. (*Wide World Photos*)

2. After the deVarona family moved to Berkeley, Donna became a member of the Berkeley Y team. By now she was a winner, even a record-setter. At 13, she went to Rome as a member of the United States Olympic Team—the youngest member ever! *(Wide World Photos).*

3. At 14, Donna set a new world record in the women's 200 medley individual in Tenri, Japan. This meet was the first of two junior high school good will swimming meets between young Japanese swimmers and two boys and two girls from the United States. *(Wide World Photos)*

4. Donna showed excellent form in the 200-yard back stroke event in the Women's Indoor Swimming Championships. She won the event, finishing in 2 minutes, 17.9 seconds. Donna no longer swam for the Berkeley Y and was hoping to join the Santa Clara team. (*Wide World Photos*)

5. At the same meet, in Sacramento, Donna's medal was admired by Ginnie Duenkel. The two girls swam almost neck-and-neck in the 100-yard back stroke. The judges awarded second place to Ginnie, first to Donna—whose time was 1 minute, 14 seconds. (*Wide World Photos*)

6. One of the great pleasures Donna found in traveling—aside from seeing so many new places—was the friends she made. Here she is with Sharon Finneran, left, at Osaka, Japan. Both girls took part in the second good will tour of Japan.

7. Donna did well in the short races in Japan, and in the 400-meter relay—she is shown here after setting a new record—but she lost the 400-meter individual medley to Sharon, who not only won the race but broke Donna's world record as well. (*Wide World Photos*)

8. Donna loved Japan, enjoyed traveling in the country, collecting souvenirs to take home to her parents, her sister and her two brothers. She also collected awards. Here she has just won the women's 100-meter back stroke finals in 1 minute, 11.2 seconds. *(Wide World Photos)*

9. Back home in Santa Clara, California, Donna models a Japanese kimono for her sister, Joanne, left, and shows some of the many mementos she brought home, as well as plaques and medals for the swimming events she won. *(Wide World Photos)*

10. For a swimmer, life is one long practice. Every day, Donna did dry land exercises and practiced the four basic swimming strokes. These are the back stroke, free style, breast stroke and butterfly. Here Donna shows the butterfly.

11. A swimmer cannot join another swimming club until a year after she has resigned from the first one. Here, Donna pulls on a jacket that shows that she has finally become a member of the famous Santa Clara Swimming Club.

12. The Women's National AAU Championships was Donna's first meet as a representative of Santa Clara. To celebrate, Donna broke her own national and American records in the 200-meter medley. (*Wide World Photos*)

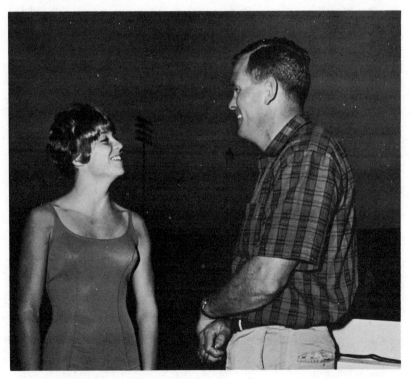

13. In the trials for the 1966 Pan-American Games, Donna broke two records, then took back the 400 individual medley record from Sharon Finneran. Above, Santa Clara coach George Haines congratulates Donna on her wins. (*Wide World Photos*)

14. In São Paulo, Brazil, for the Pan-American Games, Donna found that the South Americans very much admired both blondes and swimmers, and friendly smiles greeted her everywhere. She swam anchor laps in both relays, and the United States team won.

15. Four happy record-breakers in the senior women's indoor National AAU Championships. Donna smiles through the life preserver surrounded by, left to right, Cynthia Goyette, Michigan; Cathy Ferguson, California; Sharon Stouder, California. *(Wide World Photos)*

16. Mrs. deVarona is official keeper of the family scrapbooks that record Donna's triumphs. There are by now so many newspaper and magazine articles to clip that the whole family helps. In the picture are Mrs. deVarona, Donna, Joanne, and Kurt. (*Wide World Photos*)

17. Trying for a place on the United States Swimming Team for the 1960 Olympic Games, Donna set a new individual medley record in the 400-meter in the National AAU Championships. At 17, Donna had been in swimming competition more than five years. (*Wide World Photos*)

18. The women's 400-meter individual medley—an event of the Olympic Games in August, 1960—was won by Donna, making certain of her place on the U. S. Team. Martha Randall, left, came in second; Sharon Finneran, right, Donna's friendly rival, placed third. *(Wide World Photos)*

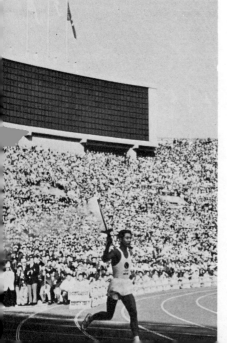

19. At the start of each Olympic Games, a torch, lighted at the site of the first games, in Greece, is carried into the stadium. Here the torch is carried by a runner into the stadium in Tokyo, Japan, to open the 1960 Olympic Games—in which Donna took part. *(Wide World Photos)*

20. At the 1960 Olympics, Donna shows off the gold medal that she won on October 17. Donna set a new Olympic record time of 5 minutes, 18.7 seconds in the women's 400-meter individual, considered one of the greatest victories of the entire games. *(Wide World Photos)*

21. The back stroke is the only one of the four basic swimming strokes used in AAU meets that is done while the swimmer is on his back. Here Donna demonstrates her swift, seemingly effortless—but powerful—back stroke, as she takes a breath.

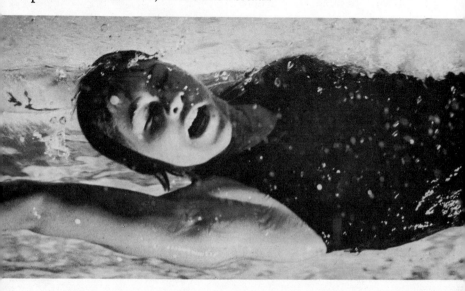

22. Shortly after the Olympics, Donna made her decision: she would give up competition swimming. She entered U.C.L.A. in the fall of 1965, pledged a sorority—Kappa Kappa Gamma—and became the coach of the university's first women's swimming team.

23. Donna became an announcer of swimming events for the American Broadcasting Company. She also works for the Antipoverty Program and is a member of the President's Council on Physical Fitness. She still swims a mile a day, to keep in shape.

Starting in October, 1959, Donna swam two hours every day in the 50-meter Treasure Island pool. She continued through the winter, pushing herself to new and better times in all events.

No longer was she swimming in the junior events; she was good enough to be in the senior races, often winning over girls several years older.

Even though her training schedule had been stepped up, Donna found she had time to do all the things she wanted to do. Every Wednesday night she returned from her work-out in time to take part in the dances at her school, Stanley Intermediate. Other days she took part in general school activities. In fact, she had more confidence in herself these days, and in her relations with her fellow students. Her success with swimming had helped her to start enjoying many things she had been a bit fearful of before.

The Berkeley YMCA decided to send a four-girl team to the Indoor National Championship at Bartlesville, Oklahoma, in April of 1960. Donna was chosen as one of the four. This would be the first time she had ventured out of California for a swimming meet, and she made up her mind to do her best. Added to this was the fact that she would be swimming against Jan and Carol Swenson.

Coach Swenson and his wife had brought their two daughters to the Oklahoma meet. The Swensons had their eyes on the Olympic try-outs in Detroit that August. Important wins in the outdoor nationals would strengthen their positions.

Donna placed fourth in the 250-yard free style and helped her team win the 400-yard relay. She also placed fourth in the 500-yard free style, scoring ahead of Jan Swenson. But the real surprise came when Donna beat Jan in the 400-yard individual, landing second place only a short distance behind the winner, Carol Swenson!

After school ended in June, Donna began all-out training for the Olympic challenge. A series of development meets for western swimmers was held at the Fremont Hills Swim and Tennis Club, and Donna entered the competition.

No one worked harder than Donna. In both the 400-meter free style and the 100-meter free style, she provided stiff competition for U.S. champion Chris von Saltza of the Santa Clara Swimming Club. So great was Donna's improvement that she cut four seconds off her 100-meter time during the meets.

Then she was faced with a decision. She discussed it with her father.

"The Berkeley Y isn't going to send a team to the outdoor nationals at Indianapolis," she told him.

"Why not?" Mr. deVarona asked.

"Coach Yamashita says he wants us to stay home and train for the Olympic trials in Detroit the following month. He thinks we will do better if we don't break up our training to go back East."

"What do you think, Liz?"

Donna's answer to that was quick and sure. "I'd like to go to the nationals. I think I need the experience in competition. Most of the girls I've been swimming against have been in more nationals than I have. Besides, I think I do better when I have something to shoot for."

"I think you are right, Liz," her father agreed, "but I wanted to hear you say it. I used to be the same in football. I'd get stale and bored by too much training, but I'd play my heart out in a game."

"But if the Berkeley Y isn't sending a team to the nationals, what can I do?"

Her father thought for a moment. "I think we can figure out something. You are still good friends with Debbie Lee, aren't you?" When Donna nodded, he said, "Good. I will call George Haines, Debbie's coach at Santa Clara, and see if you can't go along with his team."

George Haines liked the idea. Donna was becoming well known as a swimmer, and he felt she would be good competition for his girls—make them put forth extra effort. He even suggested that Donna come down to Santa Clara and work out with his team for two weeks before going to the nationals. Donna was delighted, and she arranged to stay with Debbie Lee's family in Santa Clara.

The training with George Haines was an important step forward for Donna. Santa Clara was the most famous club for girl swimmers—it was called a "champion factory." Every day Donna was swimming beside Chris von Saltza, Lynn Burke, national back stroke champion, Ann Warner, national breast stroke champion, and other great swimmers. She studied their styles and took the tips that Coach Haines offered. She could feel her strokes improving, and the results were proved on the stop watch.

One day as Debbie Lee and Donna returned home after an especially hard work-out, Mrs. Lee called from the kitchen: "There's a letter for you on the hall table, Donna. Looks important."

Donna went to the hall and picked up a large envelope with a red, white and blue stripe. "It is from the United States Olympic Committee," she said in surprise. "What do you suppose it could be?"

"Probably that you are refused a place on the team for being a poor swimmer," Debbie cracked. "Open it, silly."

Donna slit open the envelope and took out the letter. She read it aloud:

"Dear Miss deVarona:

On June 21, 1960, this office wrote to inquire of your height and weight. Since you may possibly be chosen to represent the United States in the Olympic Games at Rome, a uniform must be ordered. You gave your size as five feet two inches and 102 pounds. Before ordering the uniform, we would like to be sure that these figures are not in error. . . ."

Donna stared at Debbie. "What do you suppose that is all about?" she asked.

"Simple," Debbie replied. "They just cannot believe those figures could be correct. You see, they've never had a dwarf on the Olympic team before."

CHAPTER 8

THE WORLD'S RECORD

"Gee, I'd give anything to win this race," Donna said to Debbie Lee as she pulled on a dry swim suit. They were sitting in the locker room of the stadium in Indianapolis, where the outdoor nationals were being held. The place was filled with other girls who were waiting to swim in the afternoon events on the first day.

"You've done all right so far," Debbie pointed out. Donna had already raced in three events that day. In the morning she had swum the 100-meter free style and the 400-meter individual, and her times were good enough to place her in the finals. That afternoon she had placed third in the 100-meter finals, which indicated she would have a good chance of making the Olympic team when the trials were held in Detroit.

"But it is the 400 that means the most to me," Donna said.

"Why?" Debbie asked. "The race isn't one of the Olympic events."

"I know, but it is still my favorite race. It shows I can be good in every stroke."

Debbie smiled. "I don't suppose the fact that Carol Swenson is also swimming the 400 has anything to do with it?"

"Well, I wouldn't mind beating her," Donna admitted. "But that isn't the whole story. I just want to win that race."

The loud speaker in the corner of the locker room announced: "Next event—women's 400-meter individual."

"Oh, boy, here it is!" Donna said. She reached into her locker and took out a small metal box. She opened it and removed a pill which she popped into her mouth.

"What's that?" Debbie asked.

"A vitamin pill," Donna said.

"Do you really think it does any good before a race?"

"Probably not. It is for good luck. I always take one before a big race. Donna grinned. "Did you know I was that way about a lot of things? I have to take the first shower stall in a locker room. If it is occupied, I wait. And before every race, I count to four."

"You *are* a nut!" Debbie exclaimed.

Donna hurried out into the sunlight and walked toward the starting area. Suddenly she came face to face with Coach Swenson. Donna hadn't seen him since she defeated his daughter Jan at the indoor finals at Bartlesville. She was afraid he might be angry with her, and she didn't want him to be. She had valued his coaching, particularly his insisting on long workouts in every stroke, and she hoped they could remain friends.

She greeted him with a friendly, "Hi, Coach."

"Oh, it's you," the coach said. "How do you feel?"

"I'm really nervous," Donna answered honestly.

"Afraid you might lose this time?"

Donna went on to the starting line. Her heart was pounding, and suddenly she grew angry. When she sat down on the starting blocks, she was shaking and crying. All at once the pressure seemed too great.

"Swimmers, take your marks!"

The familiar words brought Donna back to earth, and she mounted slowly to the starting block. She gazed to the left and saw Carol Swenson standing ready. Now the race seemed impossible. Carol was a perfectly formed five feet eleven inches, a full nine inches taller than Donna. Carol was nineteen years old, six years older than Donna. She had been started in swimming by her father at a much earlier age than Donna.

She looked to her right and saw Becky Collins, the seventeen-year-old holder of the world's record for the 200-meter butterfly. Others in the race included meet winners and record holders. But Donna had no time

left to think about her competition. The race was beginning in a few seconds.

"One, two, three, four," she counted to herself, and
the starting shot rang out.

The start was clean. All eight girls hit the water at
the same moment. Immediately the pool was splashing
white from the windmill strokes of the butterfly.

Becky Collins took the lead, as expected. At the
first turn she was half a length ahead of Carol and
Donna. By the end of the butterfly she was a length
ahead. Then came the back stroke.

Now Becky was left behind as Donna and Carol
pulled ahead of her, almost neck-and-neck. Donna was
surprised to find her back stroke working so easily. It
had never been a good stroke for her, but by the end
of the first two hundred meters she had pressed in
front of Carol by a length and a half.

The breast stroke lost Donna's lead. Carol's steady
pull brought her into the lead by three-quarters of a
length, and now Becky Collins was pressing on Donna
for second place. Donna found the breast stroke the
most tiring of all; her whole body began to ache.

She took a flat-handed turn against the end of the
pool—pushing off the pool edge with the palm of her
hand as she turned—and began the final two laps in
the free style.

Becky had used up her strength. Now it became

a two-girl race—Carol Swenson and Donna deVarona. The crowd was roaring at the fury of the competition.

Donna whipped her arms through the water and began gaining on Carol. The lead had been cut to half a length as they approached the final turn.

"I've got to flip this last turn," Donna told herself. "With Carol's height, she's bound to get a better turn if she pushes off. But I could get a faster turn if I flip. Do I have enough strength left?"

She did. She flipped under water—a sort of underwater somersault—and came up to find herself even with Carol. The finish wall was getting closer and closer, and neither of them gave an inch.

"Can I do it?" Donna wondered. "I don't know, but here goes!"

She took a gulp of air, put her head down and raced through the water until she touched the wall.

Donna didn't have the strength to get out of the pool. She ached in every bone, every muscle. She felt as if she would sink to the bottom of the pool if she didn't hold on to the rope separating the lanes. She was so tired she couldn't hear the cheers of the crowd in the stadium.

"You won!" shouted Debbie Lee as she leaned over the side and offered a helping hand to lift Donna out of the pool.

"You not only won," added George Haines, who was

bending to help on the other side, "you broke the world's record by fifteen seconds!"

"I did what?"

"It is official," George Haines said, as other members of the Santa Clara team gathered around Donna. "You won in five minutes thirty-six and five-tenths seconds. You broke Carol's record."

Donna still couldn't completely believe her victory even after she heard her name over the loud speaker, even after she was given her medal. Only when she returned to her hotel did she realize what had happened. Her first clear thought was that she had to call her parents, back in Lafayette.

It seemed like a long wait before she heard her father's voice on the other end of the phone.

"Dad—guess what happened!"

"You won the 400 individual and set a new world's record," he said at once.

"Oh." Donna was disappointed. "You know already."

"Of course we know, and so does everyone else in Lafayette. It is all over the radio and TV."

"Is it really?"

"Of course! And the local paper has a big story about Donna deVarona setting a world's record."

"Honest to goodness?"

"I wouldn't kid you. And Liz—"

"Yes, Dad?"

"Your mother and I are very proud."

At last she had achieved what she had worked for all those long cold nights at the Treasure Island pool. She had been able to swim one of the toughest of all races faster than any girl ever had done before. And in so doing, she had beaten Carol Swenson and had taken the world's record away from her.

She thought about Coach Swenson. He had trained her well and had given her the will to succeed. Her father had once told her to put her mind to getting all the good she could out of Karl Swenson as a coach. It had worked.

Completely weary, Donna drifted into a deep sleep.

CHAPTER 9

THE ROAD TO ROME

During the entire time at Indianapolis, Donna tried not to think about the Olympics, because when she did those butterflies started racing around her stomach.

It was simply too much to hope for. Would she actually become a member of the 1960 Olympic team? Everything seemed to be against her. Never before had a girl swimmer made the American team at the age of thirteen. And now she was in competition entirely by herself, without the advantage of having team mates to cheer her on and a coach to give her needed instructions. George Haines was very helpful, but he had heavy responsibilities to the members of his own team, Santa Clara.

"I feel kind of on the outside," Donna said to her room mate, Debbie Lee.

"Don't feel that way," Debbie said. "We all love you, even if you aren't a Santa Claran—yet. Just think of yourself as a great big team all by yourself. That's what you are, you know. You'll be wearing the Berkeley Y colors. And you know they'll be rooting for you back there. And so will your family, even if they cannot be here."

Donna nodded. "I guess you are right, Debbie. I never thought of it that way."

And so, as she took her warm-ups on the second day of the outdoor nationals at Indianapolis, she thought of her team mates at the Berkeley Y. They all had patted her on the back and wished her success on the day she left California. She remembered waving to her mother and father as she walked up the stairs to the big jet.

"We will be pulling for you!" her father had called above the noise.

Donna pushed the thought of the Olympic Games out of her mind. She was going to do her best for her family and friends, and that was all she could do.

And she did. In spite of the exhausting races of the previous day, she finished third in the 400-meter free style. She swam the best time of her career in the 200-meter free style trials. On the following day she placed fourth in the finals.

At the closing ceremonies, the scores of the various teams in the competition were announced. Over the loud speaker came the words: "Fifth place goes to the Berkeley, California, YMCA."

The newspapers noted that the fifth place had gone

to a team that had only one member, and a thirteen-year-old at that—Donna deVarona.

Now Donna was faced with the big challenge. She had won her chance to try for a position on the Olympic team. Swimmers would earn points for each event in which they placed, and those with the highest total of points at the end of the meet would make up the Olympic team.

The trials were being held in Detroit. Donna could sense the air of excitement as soon as she arrived in the city. All of the swimmers she met were nervous as they approached the competition, and most of them were willing—in private—to admit it.

Not Donna. She couldn't really grasp the idea of flying to Europe to race in the greatest sports event of the world. The whole thing seemed completely unreal to her. "I will do my best," she told herself, "and if I lose—well, I won't cry about it. Not until I get back to my hotel room, anyway!"

She made her plans. Her best race, the 400-meter individual medley, was not in the Olympic competition. She knew her best chance for making the team was in the 100-meter free style.

"I don't think I've got a chance in the 400-meter free style," she told herself. "If I'm going to make the Olympic team, I will have to do well in the 100-meter."

She swam the 100-meter over and over again, figuring out how to pace herself during the race. She practiced her turns until every movement was smooth and easy. She realized that many a race, especially a short one like the 100-meter, could be lost by one poor turn.

On the first day of the Olympic trials, Donna swam the 100-meter free style well enough to be among the sixteen semi-finalists. That night she scored a good enough time to be one of the eight girls to swim in the finals.

She swam with all her skill, but she placed only fifth.

Donna's spirits rose when she tried out for the 400-meter free style. She became the third American girl ever to swim the race in less than five minutes. She swam even better in the final race, but placed third to Chris von Saltza and Carolyn House, who thus won their places on the Olympic team. But Donna's third did not add enough to her list of points to earn her a place.

Donna knew that only one chance remained for her to make the Olympics. She had to swim well enough to be a member of the 400-meter relay team.

Now the pressure was on. All the other girls who had failed to make the team for the Olympics were also out to do their best. Donna managed to finish second in her next-to-final heat, scoring the fourth best time among all those trying for the finals.

Then she began the long wait until the final race. Hours went by as other events were held in the big pool. While she waited for her own race to be called, Donna remembered her first big meet, the Far Western at Fleischacker Pool in San Francisco. That had been only three years before, when she was ten.

Donna remembered sitting on the lawn with her father, shivering in the gray fog as she waited. She had lost the race because she was nervous and hungry and not experienced. She had come a long way since that August day in 1957. And now, as she waited, she made up her mind to go farther still—to Rome.

"Next race—women's 100-meter for a place on the relay team."

The voice on the loud speaker brought Donna back to the present. It was 11 P.M. and time for her final chance to join the Olympic team.

The start was smooth and fast. On the first lap, Donna pushed ahead with a slight lead. But after the turn she fell back.

"I've got to make it!" she told herself. "This is my ticket to Rome."

She put forth a burst of speed and tied with two other girls for third. But that was enough—it brought her total number of points high enough to earn her a place on the Olympic team!

Donna raced to a telephone. This time she wanted to break the news before her family heard about it.

"Hi, Dad," she said. "Well, I guess I will be coming home."

Her father started to comfort her. "Well, Liz, you did your best," he said.

"I mean I will be coming home in two months—after Rome!" she shouted happily.

CHAPTER 10

ONE OF THE WORLD'S
BEST SWIMMERS

"It must have been like this in the ancient days of Rome," Donna thought.

As usual, her imagination was running away with her. But what young girl wouldn't be struck with wonder if she found herself in Donna deVarona's shoes at that moment?

There she was, outside a Roman stadium with the greatest athletes in the world, listening to the shouts of a hundred thousand persons jammed inside.

But she was not waiting to face death or triumph before a Roman emperor. She was one of the members of the 1960 Olympic teams, the finest athletes in the world. They had come across continents and oceans from scores of nations, including some that Donna had never heard of. And Donna was the youngest athlete there.

Two years before, she reminded herself, she hadn't even known what the Olympic Games were. When she had first heard about them, she had had to ask her father what they were.

"The Olympic Games began in Greece many centuries ago," Mr. deVarona had told her. "The best Greek athletes would come together every four years to take part in races and other contests. In 1896 a very wise man named Baron de Coubertin proposed starting the Olympic Games again, as a way of promoting peace and understanding among the nations of the world. Ever since then, the games have been held every four years—except when there were world wars —and they take place in different capitals of the world. The next one is in 1960 in Rome."

And now it was 1960, and here was Donna herself in Rome, chosen as one of the best swimmers of the United States.

"All right, everybody in line!" ordered the team captain. "We are about to enter the stadium. Walk smartly, keep your lines straight and your heads up. Remember—you are representing the United States of America."

Donna took her place at the end of the rows of women athletes. The women marched first, and the tallest were placed at the front, to enter the stadium first. Donna—still just five feet two inches tall and scarcely a hundred pounds when sopping wet—brought up the rear.

"Ready, march!"

Donna heard the command and started marching. She had begun with her right foot and found herself out of step with the rest of the girls, but she skipped quickly and corrected herself. She had learned to take longer strides, so she could keep up with the others.

As she passed through the tunnel that led to the stadium, she began to hear the sound of the band and the noise of the crowds. Her heart beat quickened. "I feel like a Christian being fed to the lions," she whispered to the girl ahead of her.

Then she emerged into the bright Italian sunshine and forgot all her fears. An immense roar swept down upon her, but it was not frightening. It was warm and friendly, full of admiration and affection. It came from all the thousands of people who had come to Rome from all over the world to see the games.

"This is what it means to be in the Olympics," Donna thought, striding along to keep up with the others. She had never been prouder than she was at that moment.

The U.S. team circled the red cinder track and took its place with the assembled teams of other nations. The marching music stopped, and a voice on the loud speaker made an announcement in Italian. Suddenly hundreds of doves, a sign of the peaceful intent of the games, were released from cages.

The birds swept in wide circles around the inside

of the stadium, then flew off, a whirling white cloud. A feather fluttered down at Donna's feet, and she picked it up as a souvenir.

After more announcements in Italian, which she couldn't understand, a hush fell over the immense crowd. Then they leaped to their feet and cheered. Donna strained, on her toes, to see what was happening at the tunnel entrance where she had entered with the team. But she was simply too short to see over the other athletes.

"I think you need a lift, young lady," said a voice behind her.

She turned around and looked at the first row of male athletes, who had marched into the stadium behind her. The tallest were in front, and the one who had spoken was Walt Bellamy, a basketball star who towered six feet ten inches tall.

"I can fix it so you can see," he said, and with one swift movement he lifted her to a perch on his shoulder. Now she could indeed see what was going on!

A lone athlete had entered the stadium and was racing along the track. He carried a lighted torch, just like the flame that had been used in Olympic Games since the earliest Greek times. It had been lighted weeks before in the shadow of Mount Olympus in Greece and had been carried all the way to Rome.

Now the runner was racing up the stairs to the top part of the stadium, where a large, open bowl stood.

He dipped the light into the bowl, which became alive with flame. The 1960 Olympic Games had begun.

Walt Bellamy lowered Donna to the ground as the president of the International Olympic Committee began his speech of welcome to the athletes of the world. Then he began to give the Olympic pledge. Donna, who had learned the pledge the moment she felt there was a possibility of her going to the Olympics, repeated it in a solemn voice:

"In the name of all competitors, I swear that we will take part in these Olympic Games, respecting and abiding by the rules that govern them, in the true spirit of sportsmanship, for the glory of sport and the honor of our country."

Donna thought about those words as she marched out of the stadium at the end of the ceremonies.

". . . for the glory of sport and the honor of our country . . ."

She looked toward the flag at the head of the United States team. Never in her life had she been more eager to win.

But Donna was not old enough to have gained her full strength, and in the world of sports winning comes only when an athlete is at the peak of his physical powers. It simply wasn't possible, that summer of 1960, for a girl only thirteen years old to go home from the Olympic Games with a gold medal.

Donna had done her best, so far, in the 400-meter

individual, in which she swam two lengths each of the butterfly, the back stroke, the breast stroke, and the free style. But this particular event was not part of the Olympic Games.

Instead, she was entered in the 100-meter and the 400-meter free style. Donna swam well, and had she been competing with any but the world's best swimmers, she might have won. She didn't reach the finals in the 100-meter, but for a thirteen-year-old, she did remarkably well. She did reach the finals of the 400-meter and became the fourth best woman swimmer in the world in that event. But fourth wasn't good enough for a medal.

Still, while Donna did not win any medals, the trip became the greatest experience of her life, with adventure enough to supply the family dinner table with conversation for months.

In the three weeks that the Olympic athletes were in Rome, Donna managed to get lost in the middle of the city, to join the rest of the United States team for a private audience with the Pope in Vatican City and—best of all—to make friends wherever she went. She traded pins bearing the American emblem for those of foreign athletes, and she managed to gather more pins than any of her team mates. She enjoyed dancing with the track stars in the recreation hall. The Italians, who seemed to have a special feeling for blondes, adored her. She had become widely known as the youngest athlete in the Olympics, and Italians everywhere saluted her as "bambina," their word for baby.

Then the Olympic Games were over, and the team was in the huge jet plane high over the ocean, soaring for the U.S.A. and home.

"Glad to be going back?"

Donna smiled up at the friendly face of George Haines, coach of the Santa Clara Swimming Club and the Olympic swimming team.

The coach sat down in the seat next to her. "Thinking about the games?" he asked.

"Yes," Donna admitted.

"Disappointed?"

She nodded.

"You shouldn't be," said the coach. "You should feel proud that you were a part of this team."

"Oh, I am!" Donna said. "It's just that—"

"That you wish you had done better?"

"Yes."

"Why didn't you do better, Donna?"

How many times Donna had asked herself that question! "I don't know," she said sadly. "I wanted to so much."

"What about your physical condition?" Coach Haines asked. "Were you at your best?"

She shook her head. "My stomach was upset part of the time. I think it must have been the food that didn't agree with me. After a while, I didn't eat much of anything but chocolate bars."

"What about the water? Did you drink it?"

"No, everybody had warned me not to drink the water. When it got too hot, I went over to the lunch room and asked for some ice to chew on."

The coach smiled. "That could have upset your stomach just as easily as the water."

Donna frowned. "I never thought of that," she admitted.

"You have to think of everything that might affect your condition if you are going to be a champion, Donna. That includes mental condition as well. Were you thinking of home?"

Donna nodded slowly.

"I don't wonder!" said the coach. "You were away trying out for the team the whole summer. You must really be looking forward to going home."

"Yes," said Donna. She had been thinking a great deal about her mother and father and her brothers and sister in California.

"Well, I want you to know that I'm proud of the way you swam and the way you conducted yourself. I'm sure this has been a great experience for you, one that you will remember all your life. But it can also be the beginning."

"The beginning?"

"Yes. A moment ago I said, '—if you are going to be

a champion.' You can be. Any girl who has accomplished as much as you have at your age has it within her power to go right to the top. It will mean hard work—harder than you have ever known before. But if you are willing to devote your very best efforts for the next four years, you can go to the next Olympic Games in Tokyo and come home with a gold medal."

"Do you really think so?" Donna asked.

"Yes, I do," the coach said firmly. "And I will be willing to do everything I can to help you. I would like you to train with the Santa Clara Swimming Club. But you must decide. It will be tough going, and some days you will wonder why you ever stuck with it. You will miss out on a lot of the fun that other girls will have. Only *you* can make up your mind whether it will be worth four years of hard work."

George Haines returned to his own seat in the plane, leaving Donna to think about what he had said.

She had come a long way from her first dips in the San Diego Bay, from her first strokes in the Fleischacker Pool in San Francisco. She had come all the way to the Olympic Games, and it had been a difficult, often punishing road to follow.

Now she had to face a hard question for a thirteen-year-old: was she prepared to make more sacrifices for a goal that she might or might not reach four years from now?

CHAPTER 11

"COMPLIMENTS OF ROOM 516"

The year following the 1960 Olympic Games in Rome was a difficult one for Donna. She wanted more than anything to join the Santa Clara Swimming Club, but she knew that would be too much to ask of her family. It would mean the family's moving to Santa Clara, for the towns were too far apart for Donna to travel back and forth. Her father's business was in Lafayette. Her brother David was in his last year at Acalanes High School. It wouldn't have been right to ask him to leave all his friends and activities to transfer to Santa Clara. The family had other roots in Lafayette that would make moving a burden. Besides, Donna was required by AAU rules to wait for a year before joining another swimming club. She had dropped out of the Berkeley YMCA and was swimming as an independent.

Donna worked out alone in a pool at Fremont Hills, not far from her home. Her father helped with the drills, and so did a local coach.

In June of 1961, Donna had a pleasant break. She was chosen to be one of four swimmers, two boys and two girls, aged thirteen and fourteen, to go to Japan as guests of the Japanese Government. The Japanese had been impressed by the surprising records set by Donna and other American swimmers in their early teens, and they wanted to study the way the Americans swam.

Donna, Sharon Finneran, Brooks Johnson, and Roy Saari were treated in a royal manner. Everywhere they went in Japan their pictures were taken and newspaper men interviewed them. Their swimming was recorded on movie film from every angle, so their styles could be studied and copied. The grateful Japanese presented the four swimmers with gifts on every occasion.

It wasn't all work for the traveling group. They were all lively young people; they did a lot of kidding around, and—the boys particularly—were handy with practical jokes. One day at the end of the trip, the two girls returned to their hotel room all tired out.

Donna opened the door to their hotel room. "Oh, my gosh!" she exclaimed and closed the door in horror.

"What is it?" asked Sharon. "A dead body?"

"Worse," said Donna. "Look!" She swung open the door again, and Sharon was able to see all their clothes, gifts, blankets, traveling kits—everything—piled in one huge mass in the center of the room.

101

They went in a few steps, staring helplessly at the pile.

"Who would do such a thing!" Sharon exclaimed.

Donna spotted a piece of paper and snatched it up. "Here is your answer," she said. "They left their calling card." The note said: "Compliments of Room 516." It was the room occupied by Brooks and Roy.

"We've got to get revenge," Sharon declared. "But how? And when?"

"I don't know," Donna answered slowly. "But we will—some day, somewhere."

Too soon the pleasant trip to Japan was over. Now Donna had to get ready for her third outdoor nationals, to be held in Philadelphia, at which she would have to defend her crown in the 400-meter individual medley. She felt nervous about the challenge. She lacked team training. Happily George Haines agreed to take her along with the Santa Clara team on the trip to Philadelphia. That meant she would be rooming once more with her friend Debbie Lee.

The work-outs in Philadelphia went well. George timed Donna in practice races, and he kept shaking his head when she finished them.

"Either my watch is crazy," he told her, "or you are swimming faster than you ever have."

On the morning of the first day at the nationals, Donna faced two difficult races, the 400-meter indi-

vidual medley and the 100-meter free style. She was
eager to win both. The 400 was becoming her own
particular race, since she had won it at the previous
year's nationals. And the 100-meter free style had been
her ticket to the Olympic Games. She wanted to prove
that she was capable of being the best in it.

A light summer rain was falling when George Haines
picked up Donna, Debbie Lee, and other Santa Clara
swimmers in the Volkswagen bus he used to haul
them to the stadium. Donna was the last one out to
the car.

"You are late," said Mr. Haines.

"Yes," said Donna. "I usually am."

"All right, you hop in back. But don't stick your
legs out the end, understand? That back window
might come loose."

Donna jumped into the rear of the bus and tucked
her feet under her. She didn't hear the chatter of the
other swimmers because she was thinking of her two
races for that day. Even though her recent times had
been the best she had ever made, she wasn't sure that
she was ready. She didn't know *why* her times were
better, and knowing why was important.

As she stared out the back window, Donna swam
each race in her mind, pacing herself through the four
strokes of the medley and then racing in the 100-
meters. Each turn was planned in her mind.

The bus was nearing the stadium when Donna felt a

cramp in her leg. She stretched her legs out the back window, and the cramp disappeared.

At that moment, George Haines drove through a puddle that hid a rut in the street. The bus jumped sharply and the rear window came crashing down on Donna's legs.

She cried out in pain. Mr. Haines slammed on the brakes and ran around to find the window still on her legs. He lifted it and told Donna to move her feet. The pain made her gasp.

"That bad?" he asked.

Donna nodded.

"But you can move your feet?"

Donna tried again. "Yes."

"Then I don't think any bones are broken."

Donna started to lift the legs of her sweat suit so she could look at the wound. She twisted in pain.

"Leave it alone," Mr. Haines said. "I'm taking you right back to the motel. Dr. von Saltza is there, and he can treat you."

George Haines sped back and carried Donna into her room. Dr. von Saltza, whose daughter Chris swam for Santa Clara, arrived and took a pair of scissors from his bag.

"What are you going to do?" Donna asked nervously.

"I'm going to cut the pants leg so I can get a look at the wound," the doctor said.

"Oh, no! Not my new uniform!" she cried.

"Don't worry, Donna," George Haines said. "We will get you another one."

Dr. von Saltza slit the pants up the sides and exposed the wound. Donna felt sick. The shin bone showed through, and the wound was bleeding.

"You are a lucky girl," the doctor said as he cleaned the wound. "An inch higher or lower and you would have broken the bone."

He bandaged her legs and sent for an ice pack to reduce the pain and prevent swelling. "Just stay off your feet for a day or two, and you will be all right," he ordered.

Donna shook her head. "No. I'm going to race today."

"I think not, Donna," the doctor said. "That's a serious wound."

"But if there are no broken bones, I can use my legs, can't I?" she demanded.

"Yes, but—"

"All I need are two legs and two arms. Right?"

"Donna, be sensible," Mr. Haines said. "Those legs are going to hurt very much."

"Yes, but I hurt all over after any race. So what difference is it if my legs hurt a little more?"

Both the coach and Dr. von Saltza knew Donna well enough to realize that she couldn't be talked out of racing that day. They permitted her to return to the stadium, expecting she would soon recognize she was in no condition to race.

Donna had her own reasons for insisting on racing. The winners in the nationals would be sent to Europe for a swimming tour of England, Holland and Germany. The thought of going abroad again was enough to make her forget the pain.

She made the 100-meter free style, but she didn't have the kick to do her best in the finals and she placed fourth. "I know I can do better in a longer race," she told herself.

She did. On the same day that she had come within an inch of breaking her legs, she won the 400-meter individual, setting a new world's record. Her trip to Europe was on.

The next day, she set a world's record in the 200-meter race. At the end of the meet, she was entered in the 100-meter back stroke, a race in which she had never done her best. Though her legs were better, they ached terribly. Even so, she scored second, missing the high-point honors in the meet by only one-tenth of a second.

In that same month, she went to Europe—her legs now healed—and won in the 100-meter and 200-meter back strokes. She set still another world's record in the 400-meter individual medley.

The experience at Philadelphia proved a valuable lesson to Donna. She could easily have given in to the pain and spent the nationals on her bed in the motel. She chose to treat her injured legs as small problems that had to be forgotten.

Donna realized it had to be the same way with other things. Was the pool too cold? Did she have a stomach ache? Had some other swimmer said something to upset her? No matter. The only important thing was swimming the best race she was capable of —and maybe even better than that. Such was the way of a champion.

CHAPTER 12

THE SANTA CLARA
SWIMMING CLUB

"I'm just not making it, Dad," Donna complained, as her father drove her home from the Pleasant Hills Country Club after her work-out.

"What do you mean, Liz?" he asked.

"I mean I'm not getting in shape," she said. "I can feel it. I will never be ready for the indoor nationals."

"What do you think is wrong?"

"I'm not getting enough work-outs, for one thing. Other kids are swimming ten or twelve hours a week. I'm only getting five."

"Maybe we can arrange for you to swim more at some other pool," her father suggested.

"It isn't just that. Swimming alone is no fun. I miss working out with a team. The only time I really feel like swimming is when you take me down to Santa Clara on Saturdays, and I can have some races with Debbie and the other girls. The boys, too."

"I know this year has been tough on you, Liz," Mr. deVarona said. "But your year of waiting will be over in a few months, and you'll be able to join the Santa Clara team. You'll get back in your stride then."

"But it might be too late for the 1962 season," Donna objected.

"Then there's always 1963."

"How would that be any different? I'd still be working out alone during the year."

"No, you wouldn't. I've been talking to your mother, and we've decided we would like to live in Santa Clara."

"What?" said Donna in surprise.

"Why not? Deet will be out of high school soon, and he can go to junior college down there. It won't make any difference with my work, since I travel all around the Bay area. I might as well live fifty-five miles away in Santa Clara as in Lafayette."

"Oh, Dad, that would be wonderful!" Donna threw her arms around her father's neck.

"Hey, watch that!" he protested happily. "You want me to drive off the road?"

As she expected, Donna was not at her best in the distance races at the indoor nationals in Sacramento in April, 1962. She thought she could do well in the 400-meter individual medley, but she stayed out of it. George Haines had some good swimmers in the race. She realized that if she didn't enter, they would have a better chance to score points for Santa Clara and help the team win the meet.

Donna entered the 200-meter back stroke, which she had never been in in the nationals, and the 100-meter back stroke, which she had never won. She scored first in both races. She also won the 200-meter individual medley, which was being offered in national competition for the first time.

At the end of the meet, a voice came over the loud speaker: "Winner of the team title—Santa Clara Swimming Club." Donna cheered as loudly as any of the Santa Clara members. Even though she did not belong, she had contributed to the victory by remaining out of the 400-meter individual medley and by defeating swimmers of other clubs in her three events.

Donna returned to Japan that summer. There she learned how poorly she had prepared for the swimming season. She did well in the short races, winning the 100-meter butterfly and the 100-meter back stroke, but she lost the 400-meter individual medley to Sharon Finneran. Not only did Donna lose the race—she also lost her world record, which Sharon broke.

When Donna went to the outdoor nationals in Chicago the following month, she was racing for the first time as a member of the Santa Clara Swimming Club, for the deVaronas had made the promised move. That gave her pride, and she planned to swim her best races so she could help the team's score.

"You have a lot of good girls who can swim the 100 free style," she told Coach Haines. "So why don't I stay out of it?"

"All right, Donna," he said. "What do you want to swim?"

"Why don't I start out with the 200-meter back stroke and the 400 individual medley?"

"But those races follow each other."

"Yes, but I notice there's a special event in between. That will give me a chance to catch my breath."

It turned out that the special event was not held and the two races were run back-to-back. Donna scored second place in the 200-meter back stroke. She accepted her medal and had to race back to the pool for the start of the 400-meter individual medley. She placed third—her worst performance in the race that she had considered to be her particular property.

She tried out for the two races in the morning. George Haines told her, "There's going to be a special event and a lot of other finals. You go back to the hotel and get a good rest."

Donna followed his instructions. She had always been able to sleep well before a race. "I can worry about it when I wake up," was the way she figured. She fell into deep slumber and was awakened by the arrival of a telegram.

It was from her brother David. He and Donna had always been close, and he must have realized that her spirits would be low after her performance the day before.

The telegram read: "Liz, I'm here wrapping packages in the paper factory and thinking about you all the time. I'm sorry about yesterday, but I know you are always a winner. Go get them today. I know you can do it. I love you. Deet."

Donna heard Debbie Lee's voice outside the door: "Hey, Devo, come on! We will be late for the race!"

Donna folded the telegram and put it into her pocket. She hurried down to the car where Debbie was waiting.

"Almost out of gas," said the driver as they pulled away from the hotel.

"Maybe you had better stop and get some," Donna suggested.

"No. Haven't got time. We should just about make it."

He pulled out onto the road and started toward the stadium. Donna turned on the radio and switched stations until she found some rock-'n'-roll music. That was always a good way of calming her nerves before a race.

As they pulled up in front of the stadium, Donna was surprised to see George Haines out in front. He seemed very excited. The moment he spotted them he ran toward the car. "Come on, hurry up!" he shouted. "Your race has already been called!"

Donna ran after him through the crowd. "I'm not sure we can make it," he said over his shoulder. "I did everything I could to stall the race. I even told my daughter to fall in the pool with her clothes on, if necessary."

"At least I have my suit on. That helps," Donna thought. She knew if she didn't arrive in time for this race, she couldn't swim in any of the others. Those were the meet rules.

They arrived at the starting blocks just as the starter was ready to lift his gun. Donna skinned out of her sweat suit and took her position to start. She made a false start once, to give herself time to catch her breath. Then she mounted to the starting block again and was ready for the race.

Ready, indeed! In spite of the rush to get there, Donna not only won the 200-meter individual medley, she set a new United States record!

With scarcely a chance to dry off, Donna had to report for the 400-meter relay. The Santa Clara team won the race, and Donna swam her fastest time.

On the way out of the stadium, a woman remarked to George Haines, "You've got quite an actress on your team."

"What do you mean?" he asked.

"I'm talking about Donna deVarona. That was quite an act she put on, running in late."

"Madam," said Mr. Haines with feeling, "believe me, that was no act."

When Donna reported back to the car, she found Debbie Lee there ahead of her. But no driver.

"What's up?" Donna wanted to know.

"You won't believe it—the driver has gone after gas. He ran out of gas just as we got here."

Donna whistled. "What a lucky break we did get here!"

Debbie nodded. "You can say that again. Look." She pointed to one of the rear tires.

Donna's eyes followed her pointing finger. The tire was flat. She grinned. "I will say it again, all right—what a lucky break. What a very lucky break!"

CHAPTER 13

THE PAN-AMERICAN GAMES

"Devo has had it."

"Yes, too bad. She could have really helped the team if she had started with us a couple of years ago, when she first started getting hot."

Donna heard the conversation in the next locker room. Two other girl swimmers on the Santa Clara Swimming Club were talking about her, and she knew what they meant. She had had a poor work-out that day, and the two girls were ready to consider Devo— that was what the team called her—ready to retire at the age of fifteen.

"But I'm not ready to retire!" she thought.

Donna knew that a girl swimming champion seldom stayed at the top for more than two years. That was about as much pressure as a girl could stand. Donna had seen what happened to a couple of girls who pushed themselves too hard.

Two years was about as long as a swimmer could defend her record before younger, highly trained girls came along to take her place. Besides, most team swimmers discovered there were other, more demanding interests in their early teens than swimming hundreds of laps every week. High on the list were boys.

Boys were high on Donna's list, too. She had dated several of whom she was very fond, and her father still insisted that she save Friday for date night, no matter how hard she was training.

Donna led an active life in and out of school. She served as her class president, and she had a part in the school play. But none of those things was important enough to make her consider giving up swimming to expand her social life.

"I haven't yet reached my peak as a swimmer," she told herself. "And I won't quit until I do!"

Donna knew that others shared the opinion of the two girls in the locker room. She had been doing well in a variety of events, but she still had been unable to gain back her crown in that most tiring of races, the 400-meter individual medley. She knew that until she did, her fellow swimmers would feel that she had passed her peak.

Donna trained hard for the indoor nationals to be held in Berea, Ohio, in April of 1963. For a month before the meet, she took special work-outs, ate careful meals, and went to bed at 9 o'clock every evening. By the time she arrived in Ohio, she felt as ready for competition as she had ever been. She would have to be at her best. This year the indoor nationals would also serve as trials for the Pan-American Games, to be held in Brazil the same month. That was a special prize that all the swimmers would be aiming for.

The relays were held on the first day of the meet. Donna had made up her mind to do better than her best for the team effort. And she did—she broke the American back stroke record for the 100-meter in the medley relay and swam the fastest 100-meter in the free-style relay that had ever been recorded.

She had raced with all her heart in those two events. On the second day, Coach Haines talked to her before she started the 100-meter free style.

"How do you feel, Donna?" he asked.

"I don't know, kind of nervous," she admitted.

"Well, calm down and just try to swim your best race," he said. "You don't have to break the world's record every time."

Donna couldn't calm down and swam the 100 in 55 seconds, while she had done as well as 53.8 in workouts. The judges gave her third place, even though many people thought she placed second.

Next came the 400 individual medley, and that was the race Donna had been aiming at all year. Now she would be racing against Sharon Finneran, who had taken the record away from her in Japan. Donna felt if she did not get her crown back now, she might never have another chance. She *had* to win.

But again her nerves showed. Starting out in the butterfly, Donna swallowed a gulp of water, something that swimmers dread. She was thrown off her stroke for a moment, and Sharon pushed into the lead.

Donna gained back the lead in the back stroke, but then lost it to Sharon once more in the breast stroke.

"Well, it is now or never!" Donna told herself as she flipped into the free style. Sharon was still ahead of her, but Donna put forth every ounce of strength she had and won the race by two-tenths of a second. Once more the 400-meter individual medley belonged to *her*.

But the victory didn't assure Donna of a trip to Brazil, since that race wasn't in the Pan-American Games competition. The only chance she had left was the 200-meter back stroke. It was to be raced on the last day of the nationals, after Donna had swum in the 200-meter individual medley.

She won the medley, but she wasn't at her best in the back stroke. On the third turn, she did a bad flip and her feet landed in the gutter. She finished third.

Donna was upset at the end of the meet.

"What's the frown for?" Coach Haines asked her.

"You saw my races," she replied.

"You won the high-point prize! You scored more than any other girl in the nationals. How can you be unhappy about that?"

"Because I could have done better. And now I don't get to go to the Pan-American Games."

"I have news for you," the coach said with a smile. "You *are* going. Your time in the 100 free style was good enough for a place on the relay teams."

That helped.

"There's nothing wrong with being a relay swimmer, even though it is better for the spirit to win your own race alone," the coach went on. "I'd like to see you go down to Brazil and swim the best relays of your life."

Donna did just that. She swam the anchor laps—the last swimmer on the team—in both relays, and the U.S. team won both races.

Seeing South America was a new and thrilling experience for Donna. She found that the Brazilians, like the Italians, adored blondes, and she was greeted with friendly smiles wherever she went. Sharon Finneran was on the trip, and she and Donna decided they had to see Rio de Janeiro. So they took a plane from São Paulo, where the games were being held, to Rio.

The sight of Rio de Janeiro from the air took Donna's breath away. There was the lovely curve of beach, the beauty of Sugar Loaf Mountain, the huge statue of Christ on Corcovado Peak.

The two girls felt a charge of excitement as they stepped out of the jet plane into the bright sunshine of Rio. They carried their gear into the air-port's main building, which was alive with the sound of music coming over the loud speaker. Donna asked at the desk about hotel rooms.

"Impossible, miss," the clerk answered. "This is the time of the year when we have many visitors and there isn't a hotel room in all of Rio."

"What will we do?" Donna asked Sharon. "Sleep on the beach?"

Sharon laughed. "Lucky for us—I have an uncle who lives here. I'm sure he will be able to take care of us."

Sharon's uncle worked some kind of magic, and the "impossible" hotel room was quickly secured. Once Donna and Sharon were recognized as swimming champions from the United States, they were given the best of treatment—including dinner on a roof-top restaurant that looked over the full sweep of Copacabana Beach.

Next day, all shining and refreshed, Donna and Sharon returned to São Paulo for the finish of the meet.

But before leaving for the United States, they had some unfinished business to take care of. Also at the meet were Brooks Johnson and Roy Saari, the boys with whom they had toured Japan. Donna and Sharon still smarted under the memory of what Brooks and Roy had done to their hotel room.

"We have to do the same thing to them," Donna insisted. "It is the only way to get even."

"But how?" Sharon asked. "They live in a dormitory

with a lot of other boys. You've heard how boys walk around dormitories with nothing on. It could be a bit embarrassing if we sneaked in."

"I have an idea. Maybe one of the coaches would join us in the plot. Then he could tell us when the dormitory would be empty, and we could get in and do our dirty work."

The plot worked. A helpful coach advised the girls when they could enter the dormitory without being seen. When Brooks and Roy returned from their final races, they found their room turned upside down. Pants legs were tied in knots; clothes, blankets, pillows were piled in one great mess.

On top of the pile was a short note: "Revenge from Room 515."

CHAPTER 14

ONE MORE CHALLENGE

The year 1964 brought great pressure to bear on Donna deVarona. It was the Olympic Games year, when every athlete was straining to perform his best. Donna was faced not only with the physical necessity of training to win, but with other problems as well.

Being very friendly by nature, Donna wanted everyone to be her friend. But she found this wasn't possible when in competition with others. She knew what other girls were saying about her.

"The TV people just love Donna. Every time they show a meet, they wait until Donna races, and they interview her when she wins. What about the other swimmers? . . ."

"Who does she think she is, trying to swim every event? If she wanted to be a one-girl swimming team, why did she join Santa Clara? . . ."

But the men from the newspapers, magazines, and TV were more interested in Donna than in the other swimmers. She was bright and pretty and made good copy. At sixteen, she was already well known in the swimming world. She was a "star."

As for swimming so many different events, the variety of races, short and long, offered a challenge to her. She met the challenge by behaving the only way she knew how—by doing her best.

Before she had joined Santa Clara, she had sometimes stayed out of races so that George Haines could build up his team score. But now that she was part of the team, it made no sense not to enter events that she had a good chance of winning.

Donna was learning all the ways to be a champion swimmer, including how to gain an advantage in races. It was something that swimmers seldom talked about to each other, but each had his own tricks.

With Donna it was a system of studying the strokes of the swimmers she would race against, to learn their strong and weak spots. Then she would plan her own race pattern accordingly. She knew her own weak spots and tried to make up for them during the race.

An important feature of gaining an advantage over the other swimmers came when the girls lined up at the beginning of the race. Sometimes Donna found the best plan was to appear nervous and worried about the race. This could upset the others and make them jumpy.

More often, Donna was simply very calm about the race. She made jokes. She laughed. She yawned. Actually, this was quite natural, because she usually *was* calm before racing. This calmness often was more upsetting to the other swimmers than any nervousness.

Donna trained very hard through the winter, and in March of 1964 she traveled to Lima, Peru, for an international meet. There she was pleased to discover that the training was paying off. Once more she broke the world record in the 400-meter individual medley.

The indoor nationals were coming in April, and Donna pushed herself even harder in her work-outs. When she arrived for the meet in Pittsburgh, she was in the best condition of her swimming career.

"What else do you want to race besides the medleys, Devo?" Coach Haines asked.

"The butterfly," Donna answered.

"The butterfly? That's not exactly your stroke, is it?"

"It hasn't been," she admitted. "That's why I want to try it."

"All right," the coach said. "But we are counting on you for the relays, too. Do you think you can swim all those races?"

"Yes," said Donna. "I really can—try me and see."

She planned to live up to her reputation as the best all-around swimmer in competition. And she did. She won the 200-meter butterfly. She breezed to victory in the 200-meter and 400-meter individual medleys. And she swam on three winning relay teams!

Only one challenge remained, the 100-meter butterfly.

Donna felt the familiar ache as she stood on the starting block, shaking her arms to ease the muscles. It was the ache that had become a part of her life in the past five years. It was not exactly pain, because it was full of pleasant memories of all the races she had won.

"Swimmers, take your marks."

Donna began to ready herself for the take-off. This race was important to her, as important as the individual medleys. She needed a win in the 100-meter butterfly to score a clean sweep in all her races.

The gun sounded and Donna was off the block with a clean start. Her stroke was moving swiftly and evenly, and she quickly pulled ahead of the other swimmers.

She made a good turn, but then something happened. To the cheering crowd, it seemed that she was continuing her smooth race, but Donna knew that she was losing her stride. She simply didn't have the strength to maintain the pace she had set in the first lap.

She could sense the other swimmers gaining on her, but she thought she could bring forth a burst of speed to finish in front. She tried, but she just couldn't make it. That final burst of speed simply wasn't in her. Her lead became smaller; and then it disappeared.

Donna lost the race by one-tenth of a second.

George Haines was heading for the locker rooms when he came across Donna sitting on a bench. She was crying.

"What is this?" he asked.

She couldn't answer. Her body was shaking with sobs.

"Hey, Devo!" he said. "Is that the way a champion behaves at the end of a meet?"

Donna was finally able to talk. "I'm sorry," she said.

"Sorry for what?" the coach asked.

"Sorry because I lost the 100 butterfly."

He looked at her in surprise. "Are you out of your mind?" he demanded. "Who is the high-point winner, same as last year, I ask you? It is none other than Devo, the weepy winner! You've won three hard races and helped win three relays. And you are sorry! I wish everybody I ever coached could be so sorry!"

"But I could have won the 100 butterfly!" she insisted.

"Yes, and you might have won the 100 free style and the 30-meter side stroke," he said. "But you didn't. You might have entered a track meet and won the 100-yard dash! But it doesn't matter. You cannot win every race you enter. It is not possible. Do you want to be a swimming machine?"

"No," she said, wiping the tears from her eyes.

"Then stop pushing so hard. Sure, I like to see you win. It makes the team look good, and therefore I

126

look great. But I care more about *you*, not just about winning races. And if swimming is not going to be fun for you, I think you ought to quit."

Coach Haines lifted Donna to her feet and pushed her in the direction of the girls' locker room. "Now go get your shower and come out looking like a girl, not a swimming machine," he told her.

Donna walked into the dressing rooms, which were nearly empty now. She took her shower and got dressed. Then she stood awhile in front of the mirror. She looked at her face and recognized that she was tired. She ran a comb through her hair.

"What can you do with straight, short, stupid, swimmer's hair!" she thought, studying her damp bob. Instead of combing it straight, like a boy's, she tried to curl it at the ends.

She worked for several minutes on her hair—something she had never done in a locker room before.

On the plane returning to California, Donna stared out the window at the flat country stretched out under the cool moonlight. She thought about the nationals and how far she had come in the five years since she had first entered them at Redding, California. Then her father had had to drive her to the meet and arrange for her to stay with a friend. This time, she had traveled to and from the nationals in a jet airplane and had won more points than any other swimmer for two years running. It had been a thrill to hear the cheers of the crowd as she stepped up to accept her medals.

But was it worth all she had gone through?

As she stared through the window, Donna made up her mind that she was never again going to look behind, either at her own past performance or at the swimmers who were racing in back of her.

"From now on," she decided, "I'm not going to try to be the champion of everything. There is no meaning to that. I'm going to swim my own way, the way that pleases me. And I will swim the races that I like to swim, nothing more. And when the time comes that it isn't fun any more, then I will quit."

CHAPTER 15

GOLD MEDALS

"All right, deVarona, let's see what you can do in the back stroke this time," shouted the Olympic coach.

Donna lifted herself off the bench without her usual spring. She was working out in a Los Angeles pool, along with the rest of the swimmers who had a chance for the Olympic Games in Tokyo. Donna herself had won her usual position in the 400-meter individual medley at the trials in New York, and she had once again broken the world record doing so. She had also placed in the 100-meter butterfly and the 400-meter free style relay.

As she approached the pool for some laps in the back stroke, somebody called, "Hey, Devo!" It was her friend Debbie Lee.

"Hi, Debbie," Donna replied.

"You look like you're dragging," Debbie said.

"Oh, I will get through it all right."

"I never saw you worn out in practice before. What's the matter?"

Donna sighed. "Nothing much. It's just that the coach thinks I'm a work horse."

"And he's right."

"Maybe so," Donna said. "But I never worked like this before."

"So you have to put out a little more," Debbie encouraged. "That never bothered you before."

"No, it didn't. But now I'm not so sure it is worth it all."

"Come on, Devo!" Debbie slapped her on the back. "You are going to Tokyo! This is what you've been aiming for. You've spent four years of your life for this."

"I know, I know. It's just—well, it used to be *fun*, and now it's all work."

"Gee, Devo, I never thought I'd see the day when you thought swimming was work," Debbie said.

Donna would never have thought it, either. But she had been training a solid year for the Olympics. She knew in her heart that she was sick of getting up on the starting blocks and trying to plan how to beat the other swimmers. She was sick of the smell of pools and of wearing her hair short—sick of everything.

"This is the greatest team I have ever seen. I think it may be the greatest that has ever been assembled."

Donna had heard Olympic coach Payton Jordan use these words about the U.S. team at Tokyo. She felt proud to be part of it. Four years before at Rome, she had been excited by the spectacle of the games. Now she felt a thrill to be a real member of the American team. Then she had been only thirteen and had swum in competition for scarcely more than a year. She couldn't really grasp the importance of what was happening around her.

Now she was seventeen, and she had been racing for more than five years. The tired feeling of swimming race after race disappeared as she faced the excitement of the Olympic Games.

She loved being in Japan, which brought back fond memories of her two previous visits. Most of all, she loved the feeling of friendship she had with all the other athletes on the U.S. team.

One day Donna returned to the Olympic Village after winning a trial for the 100-meter butterfly. She walked into the recreation room and heard someone say, "Good going, Donna!"

She turned around to see tall, handsome Bill Bradley, the basketball star from Princeton University.

"That was a swell race you swam," he said.

Donna smiled her thanks.

"We all watched it on TV over there," Bill added, pointing to the color set. "We are proud of you for breaking the Olympic record."

Others came around to talk to Donna. As the games progressed, she became friends with dozens of athletes.

When she wasn't swimming, she sat with them before the TV set, and they cheered themselves hoarse as they watched the Americans pile up victory after victory.

The biggest thrill came in the 10,000-meter track race, in which no American had ever placed better than sixth. The favorite was Ron Clarke of Australia, whose best time was almost a minute better than that of the American runner, Billy Mills.

Billy was a Marine lieutenant, half Sioux Indian, from South Dakota. While he was well liked in the American section of the Olympic Village, no one really expected him to do much in the race.

But as Donna and the other Americans watched the screen, they saw Billy putting forth a burst of speed to catch up with Clarke, who had gained his expected lead.

Billy started passing a group of runners who were behind Clarke. But as he did, a runner gave him an elbow shove that sent Billy stumbling to the edge of the track.

The TV viewers gasped. Then a cheer went up as Billy resumed his stride, racing after Clarke and a Tunisian runner, who had now taken the lead.

"Come on, Billy! You can do it!" cried Donna, and everyone else in the recreation room was cheering him on.

With what seemed like a miracle, Billy Mills

pumped his weary legs until he passed the Australian and then the Tunisian and staggered across the finish line, the winner by three yards. The U.S. athletes in the recreation room, Donna included, leaped up and down and hugged each other in triumph.

Donna fell ill with a bad cold. She was unable to swim for three days, and when she raced the 100-meter butterfly, she finished fifth.

Next came the 400-meter individual medley. She wanted to break her own world record with a time that wouldn't be bettered for years to come.

Donna made a smooth start, and her butterfly was in good form. Through years of training, she could almost time herself in the various strokes. She knew that if she could maintain the pace she was setting in the butterfly, she would set her world record.

Her turns were going perfectly, and the two back stroke laps were swift and well done. Next came the breast stroke, which was always Donna's slowest.

Her lead was reaching to half the pool's distance, and the crowd was roaring over her surprising performance. But Donna realized that the lead over the others might wipe out her hopes of setting the new world record. She was half afraid that without a swimmer pushing behind her, she might shift into a kind of second gear.

She did her best with the breast stroke and then

swam the free style with all the energy she had left. Her fears turned out to be groundless. She pulled off one of the greatest victories of the entire games, and she set a new Olympic record of 5 minutes 18.7 seconds. She had won her first gold medal in the Olympic Games!

Next she was faced with the 400-meter free style relay. She would be racing 100-meters in the relay, and it was a race in which she had never been a champion. She wanted more than anything to do well in that race.

Finally the day arrived for the relay. Donna felt the familiar fluttering in the pit of her stomach as she stood behind Sharon Strouder, the first swimmer in the relay. The feeling grew stronger as the pistol cracked and the race began.

Donna watched as Sharon cut through the water with her usual strong stroke. The turn was perfect, and she came racing back a length ahead of the closest swimmer. Sharon touched the side of the pool, and Donna was in the water. Her stroke was going evenly, just as she had hoped.

Her turn was excellent, and Donna could see that she had extended the lead established by Sharon. She continued churning through the water until she felt the edge of the pool under her hand.

She leaped out of the pool and added her voice to the cheering for the last two swimmers, Kathy Ellis and Pokey Watson. Donna's team won by two lengths, setting a new Olympic record of 4 minutes and 03.9 seconds.

As Donna stood on the platform to accept her second gold medal, she felt an even greater thrill than she had felt the first time. She had won the 400-meter individual medley all on her own, and it had been the result of all those lonely hours of practice in dozens of pools from the Berkeley YMCA to the Santa Clara Swimming Club.

But she had helped win the 400-meter free style relay as part of the team, and that somehow meant more to her.

CHAPTER 16

LOOKING AHEAD

"Oh, boy, here it comes!"

Donna had tried to prepare herself for what would happen when the U.S. team marched out of the tunnel and into the Tokyo stadium for the closing ceremonies of the eighteenth modern Olympic Games. But even though she knew what was coming, she never expected it would be so great.

As the Americans stepped out into the brilliant lights of the stadium, a hundred thousand people broke out in one huge cheer. It was a vast show of affection and admiration for a magnificent team. To Donna, it was like being swept over by a wave of love.

There were thousands of Americans in the stadium, but the Japanese and others, too, joined in the cheering. They saluted the surprising achievements of the Americans, who had won thirty-six gold medals. The Russians, who had led in the previous two Olympics, had won only thirty.

Among the U.S. athletes were many whose achievements would go down in Olympic history . . . Billy Mills, who proved that Americans could win distance races . . . Bill Bradley and the rest of the basketball team; who had beaten Russia in the finals, 73–59 . . . Don Schollander, the swimmer from Oregon who had won four gold medals—more than any other swimmer in Olympic history.

Indeed, the American swimmers' performance was hard to believe. They won nine of the twelve men's events, and seven of the ten women's events—sixteen gold medals out of a possible twenty-two!

The Americans took their place on the field, along with the athletes of ninety-four other nations. Finally, the Japanese host team marched in to join them, and the closing ceremonies began.

Four years before, when Donna had stood on that other playing field in Rome, she had felt the thrill of the occasion but had not taken in its entire meaning.

She did so now. She felt the charge of excitement as the lights of the stadium lowered, and the Japanese girls who were lined up around the edge of the field began waving their torches back and forth in time to the band music. The audience hushed, and Donna began thinking about the past—and the future.

She had come a long way from that cold, hungry day at Fleischacker Pool when she was ten and completely new to competition. She remembered the chilly, tiring work-outs at Treasure Island with the Berkeley

YMCA and how Coach Swenson had pushed her into doing her best. He had taught her many good lessons. Through his training, she had learned to push herself not in just one stroke or one event, as most girls did, but in a variety of races. In so doing, she had known the challenge of attempting all four swimming strokes, and the satisfaction of becoming expert and often champion in them.

Donna remembered the triumphs and the disappointments at the nationals over the years. She had seen more of the world in her seventeen years than most people did in a life time. She had been three times to Japan, and she had been twice to Europe and twice to South America.

She thought fondly of the Santa Clara Swimming Club and especially of the wise, friendly coaching of George Haines. Donna thought, too, of her parents and was close to tears as she remembered the sacrifices they had made for her swimming career. Year after year, her mother had arisen before dawn to cook her a hot breakfast before work-outs, and there had always been a special dinner ready when she came home late from practice. When the miles her father had driven Donna to practices and meets were added together, they amounted to many thousands.

Now, as the torches of the Japanese girls flickered out, all eyes turned toward the one torch that was still burning brightly on top of the stadium.

"In a couple of minutes that flame, too, will go out," Donna thought, "and so will my swimming career."

She had made her decision. It was something she had thought about all through the difficult year preceding these Olympic Games. How much longer did she want to continue?

It made no sense to her that she should keep swimming until new stars came along and she would start taking second and third place and losing the records which she had worked so hard to set. She had seen girls do that in competition. They continued racing long after they were able to win.

"I don't want that," Donna told herself, watching the torch. "I've enjoyed swimming too much to let it grow stale. I want to quit while I'm still on top, when I can still win races. And I will never be more on top than I am at this moment."

There was scarcely a sound in the vast stadium as two hundred thousand eyes stared at the flame that was beginning to grow smaller at the rim of the stadium. It became a flicker and then it disappeared, and the stadium was in complete darkness.

Then the flood lights came on, and the audience and the athletes gave the last great cheer of the Tokyo Olympics. Donna and the other Americans began hugging and kissing each other and leaping and shouting just for the joy of a wonderful experience.

For Donna there was no sadness about her decision.

She had known rare adventure and the thrill of being a champion. Now she could go on to other experiences which she hoped would be just as thrilling.

Donna deVarona swam in one more meet, which she had already agreed to. She went to Germany in February, 1965, and won the 200-meter and 400-meter individual medleys. She was convinced that competition was no longer for her, and that was the end of her swimming career.

Now she moved on to other things.

In the fall of 1965 she entered U.C.L.A. Soon she was as active in a variety of things as she had been in swimming. She became a member of Kappa Kappa Gamma Sorority and of the Bruin Belles, the honor group of girls who stir up school spirit. She began coaching the U.C.L.A. women's swimming team. She worked at several jobs, including modeling swim suits for White Stag and helping to promote Cascade Swimming Pools and Nease Chemicals. And she announced swimming events for ABC-Television's "Wide World of Sports."

But to her the most important work came in the summer of 1966, when she served in the Antipoverty Program for the President's Council on Physical Fitness.

Donna and track star Wilma Rudolph formed "Operation Champ"—they visited Watts in Los Angeles, Harlem in New York, Chicago, Baltimore, Detroit, St. Louis and other places where there were slums, going into the poor districts to teach track and swimming in playgrounds or wherever children gathered.

One day in Baltimore, Donna went to one of the poorest sections in the city. She was to give her usual talk about the history of swimming and the development of the different strokes. But when she arrived at the "playground," she discovered there was no pool and very little ground to play on. The area consisted of a small basketball court, a couple of swings and a slide, and a wire fence to climb on. Beyond the fence were the dirty back yards of the old buildings where most of the people in the area lived.

"Hey, any of you kids know how to swim?" Donna asked a group of boys and girls who were standing around on the cement. They came closer to listen, but Donna got no sense of a friendly feeling from them. Still, she continued talking, asking their names and questioning them about their schools and sports.

When a few girls started a basketball game, Donna asked, "Can I join?"

They allowed her to join one of the teams. But as they played, Donna found that no one ever threw her the ball. Finally she grabbed it on a bounce and sank it for a basket.

Several boys of seventeen or eighteen had gathered to watch the game, and they cheered Donna's shot. But still her team mates refused to shoot in her direction. She caught the ball once more and made a basket.

"Give Whitey the ball!" shouted one of the boys on the side lines.

Donna caught another bounce and tried a shot, but an opposing player stopped her. The whistle blew.

"Foul!" said another young Negro boy. "Two free throws."

Donna aimed the ball for the basket, but missed her throw. The whistle blew once more.

"You stepped over the white line," the boy told one of the opposing players. "Take the free throw over."

By the end of the game, Donna was an accepted member of the team, and all the players called her Donna, not "Whitey."

Donna continued on her tour to other cities, but in a couple of weeks she returned to Baltimore. She made a point of returning to the tiny playground where she had played basketball. She found the same group of girls there. She walked up to them, but they moved away until she started calling them by their names.

"How come you remember my name?" asked one of the girls.

"Now, Gabriella," Donna smiled, "how could I forget that hook shot you used in the game?"

Soon the girls were sitting around her as she talked to them about their school work and the mistake of dropping out. She told them about the fun of going out for sports and trying to do their best.

"You know, anything can happen in this country," she said. "You could even go to the Olympic Games, as Wilma Rudolph and I did."

By the time she left that afternoon, Donna had made a dozen good friends and perhaps, she told herself, she had convinced some of them to remain in school and work to do their best, either in their school work or in athletics, or both.

"This is important," thought Donna, "just as important as winning in the Olympics—maybe more."

J22